THATCHER'S BRITAIN

A GUIDE TO THE RUINS

Gerald Scarfe

THATCHER'S BRITAIN

BRITAIN

A GUIDE TO THE RUINS

Original concept and initial research by
David Keys

Written and researched by
Graham Allen, Liz Atkins, Dick Barry, Bert Clough, Sean Creighton, Mike Gapes, Roy Green, David Keys, Tim Lamport, Jim Murphy, Jenny Pitkin, Martin Plaut, Gordon Prentice, Adam Sharples, Nick Sigler, Andy Thompson.

Research coordinated by
Adam Sharples

Pluto Press and New Socialist

First published in May 1983 by Pluto Press Limited,
The Works, 105A Torriano Avenue, London NW5 2RX
in association with *New Socialist*

Copyright © David Keys
and Labour Party Research Department 1983

ISBN 0-86104-713-3

Designed by Mikki Rain
Cover drawing by Steve Bell

Typeset by Grassroots Typeset, London NW6
Printed and bound in Great Britain by
Richard Clay (The Chaucer Press) Limited, Bungay,
Suffolk

Graham Allen, Liz Atkins, Dick Barry, Bert Clough,
Sean Creighton, Mike Gapes, Roy Green, Tim Lamport,
Jim Murphy, Jenny Pitkin, Martin Plaut, Gordon
Prentice, Adam Sharples, Nick Sigler, and Andy
Thompson are researchers for the Labour Party.

David Keys is a journalist and active member of the
Labour Party.

New Socialist is the Labour Party's bi-monthly
discussion magazine, independent of the party
line. Available from main newsagents and
radical bookshops.

Contents

Chris Madden

Acknowledgements

We would like to thank all those at Pluto and the *New Socialist* who have worked to impossibly tight schedules to produce this book; particularly Mike Kidron whose editorial guidance has been invaluable. Special thanks are also due to Andrew Bryan for his work on Mrs Thatcher's Diary, the references and the index, and to all those individuals and organisations who have provided information.

There is an alternative.
The Tory record is only half the story. Read about the other half—the socialist alternative—in:

Labour's Programme 1982. £1.95
New Hope for Britain (Campaign Document). 95 pence
Partners in Rebuilding Britain. 40 pence

Available post free from: Literature Sales, Labour Party, 150 Walworth Road, London SE17 1JT

Introducing Thatcher's Tories

'*The Conservative government's first job will be to rebuild our economy and reunite a divided and disillusioned people.*'

Conservative manifesto, 1979

The Tories came to power in May 1979 on a promise of lower taxes, more jobs and new opportunities. Their record in office is one of unparalleled failure. Never before has a government done so much damage to the country in so short a time:

They delivered:

- The *worst level* of unemployment ever seen in this country.
- The *biggest slump* in industry for 60 years.
- A *record* number of companies going bust.
- The *lowest* level of peacetime housebuilding since the 1920s.
- The *heaviest* tax burden ever imposed.
- The *fastest* drop in living standards since the war.
- The *greatest* raid ever on our future: investment in people and plant.

There's no excuse: Britain's is the worst economic and social record of any major country, despite the North Sea oil bonanza.

Margaret Thatcher's government is run by a new breed of Tories. Gone is any pretence at consensus, any semblance of caring for the poorest and weakest in society. Gone is the commitment to full employment that had guided governments since the war.

A new breed

The new Tories who have taken over the Conservative party seem intent on turning the clock back—to the economics of the 1930s and social values of the Victorian age.

This is what they stand for:

Free market economics

'Bringing down the rate of inflation can only be done by restricting the money supply; and doing that inevitably causes difficulties for business and rising unemployment. The high level of unemployment is evidence of the progress we are making.'

Nicholas Ridley, now a Treasury Minister,
26 January 1981

The new Tory economics is often called 'monetarism' because they see control of the money supply as the route to inflation-free prosperity. But behind all the jargon lies a simple, and familiar, purpose. They have set out to 'crash' the economy in the belief that high unemployment is the only way to cut the bargaining power of working people and get power—and profits—back into the hands of employers.

That much we have seen. But how do they get the crashed economy back on the road again? That is where the great myth of the market comes in. Keep government out. Let the weakest go to the wall. And the new climate of free market discipline, together with bigger 'incentives' for managers, will activate a hive of busily competing companies. That we have yet to see.

The worship of wealth

'The pursuit of equality is a mirage. Opportunity means nothing unless it includes the right to be unequal.'

Margaret Thatcher, 16 September 1975

'No-one would remember the Good Samaritan if he'd only had good intentions. He had money as well.'

Margaret Thatcher, 6 January 1980

Margaret Thatcher's philosophy is the unashamed defence of inequality and privilege, preaching sacrifice from the pulpits of wealth. For the Tories inequality provides incentives—a ladder for the privileged to climb, conveniently extended by handouts to the rich.

The poor must then rely on what charity they receive from the rich or from the state. But the safety net provided by the welfare state must not be too secure. To remove the fear of falling, would dull the incentive to climb.

The glories of empire

'What I favour is... a British Empire that took both freedom and the rule of law to countries that would never have known it otherwise.'

Margaret Thatcher, 17 February 1983

'If we were to sacrifice defence to the needs of the welfare state the day might come when we should have neither peace nor freedom.'

Margaret Thatcher, 17 November 1982

While we are told that children must share school books, and hospital wards must close, because the country 'cannot afford' such services, spending on weapons multiplies. The Tories have given new stridency to the rhetoric of the cold war, eagerly accepting President Reagan's dangerous new cruise missiles and boosting our own military spending far beyond that of other European countries.

Victorian values

Brian Walden:
'You've really outlined an approval of what I would call Victorian values.'

Margaret Thatcher:
'Oh exactly. Very much so. Those were the values when our country became great.'

Weekend World, 16 January 1982

Margaret Thatcher yearns for the values of Dickensian Britain, an age in which education rested on philanthropy and health care on charity. In which the absence of rights at work left employers free to exploit workers in appalling conditions. In which women knew their place and were denied the vote. In which class divisions were wide and unbridgeable.

3

Private virtues, public vices

'We have done more to roll back the frontiers of socialism than any previous Conservative government.'
Margaret Thatcher, 8 October 1982

To the new Tories the public sector is a threat. It shows that health care, education, and housing can be provided where people *need* it, not just when they can afford it. It shows that services can be subject to democratic decisions not just individual choice. It shows that organisations can be run—and run efficiently—without private profits being creamed off. To show these things is to threaten the market myths of the new Tories.

The government has attacked the public sector from every side. Cutting spending on services. Giving tax handouts to private health and education. Asset stripping valuable resources. Allowing private operators to take over the profitable areas of activity. Forcing local authorities to sell off their housing stock. Throwing the burden of caring for the old, sick and disabled onto the family and charity.

Their work is far from finished. Another five years of Thatcher could leave us with skeleton public transport, a flag day health service and supermarket schooling.

The strong state

In the name of individual freedom, the Tories have attacked rights at work and in the community, strengthening the hand of big business and the forces of the state.

They promise the earth

'Another Labour accusation is that the Tories plan to increase unemployment. But we Tories believe in policies that will create real jobs.'
Margaret Thatcher,
23 April 1979

... and deliver dust

Unemployment has gone up by two million since the Tories took over.

'We shall abolish the earnings rule that penalises so many pensioners.'
Margaret Thatcher,
1 May 1979

The earnings rule has not been abolished.

'Our plans for cutting government spending and borrowing will lower (mortgage rates).'
Tory manifesto, 1979

In January 1980 the mortgage rate was raised by 3.5 per cent to an all-time high of 15 per cent. In the last four years, it has averaged 13.3 per cent. Under Labour, it averaged 10.7 per cent.

'The Labour Party have said we are committed to putting up the price of school meals by 10p. We have no such commitment.'
Mark Carlisle,
26 April 1979

The price of school meals was put up 10p within nine months of the Tories taking office.

'Much of our higher education has a worldwide reputation for its quality. We shall seek to ensure that this excellence is maintained.'
Tory manifesto, 1979

Spending on higher education has been cut drastically, resulting in a loss of about 4,000 teaching staff.

'We have no intention to raise prescription charges.'
Margaret Thatcher,
18 April 1979

The Tories have raised prescription charges by 600 per cent, from 20p to £1.40 per item.

'Let me make it clear: the Conservative Party has no plans for new NHS charges.'
Margaret Thatcher,
18 April 1979

In October 1982 new charges were introduced for overseas visitors.

'We will cut the tax on work. We will cut the tax on savings. We will cut the tax on extra skill and effort.'
Margaret Thatcher,
25 April 1979

Taxes have been increased by the Tories—the average worker is paying over £6 a week more tax than he or she would have under Labour's tax rates.

'We have absolutely no intention of doubling VAT.'
Sir Geoffrey Howe,
21 April 1979

The basic rate of VAT was increased from 8 per cent to 15 per cent on 15 June 1979.

'There is no commitment whatsoever to abolish the Price Commission.'
Francis Pym,
23 April 1979

The Price Commission was abolished in July 1979.

'We are committed to the maintenance of a strong and effective regional policy.'
Margaret Thatcher,
26 April 1979

Regional aid has been cut back by 44 per cent and the map of the regions redrawn to cut assistance to many areas.

The new depression

Britain has entered a new depression. Tory policies have produced the biggest economic slump in sixty years. Unemployment is now higher than in the 1930s. All over the country factories stand silent and empty. There is no up-turn in sight.

In 1979 the country had a chance to make good. Unemployment had been falling for two years. Inflation was below 10 per cent. Living standards had risen by 17 per cent in two years. Industry was growing steadily and was more competitive than it had been for years.

Above all, we had black gold in the North Sea. We were about to become self-sufficient in oil—giving us an advantage over countries dependent on energy imports. We had a real chance to make the 1980s a decade of prosperity.

Instead:

- Unemployment has risen by two million.
- Production of wealth has fallen by 4 per cent.
- Output of manufacturing industry has fallen by 19 per cent.
- Investment in manufacturing has fallen by 36 per cent.
- Industry has become at least *20 per cent* less competitive.

How has this happened? A favourite Tory excuse is that we are trapped in a world recession. True, there is a world slump—the worst for fifty years. But that does not explain why Britain's record—with our oil riches—is by far the worst in the industrial world. Norway, Austria and Japan have an unemployment rate below 3 per cent; Britain's is 13 per cent, worse than any western country apart from Spain. Our crisis—unlike the goods in our shops—is 'Made in Britain'. It is a direct result of the Tory government's policies. They have set out to curb inflation by stifling industry. They have done this by:

- **Cutting public spending** – That means less spending throughout the economy and lower orders for industry. In fact, longer dole queues have in the end forced up public spending. But this only partly compensates for lost buying power. Having destroyed jobs, the government has to pay to keep people out of work.

● **Pushing up taxes** — People have less to spend if the government takes a bigger slice in tax. Under the Tories the tax burden is higher than it has ever been.

● **Raising interest rates** — Tory tight money policies pushed interest rates to an all-time high in 1980. That means businesses can't afford to borrow to invest or to hold stocks.

● **Pushing up the exchange rate** — A strong pound blocks exports and subsidises imports. So exports have stagnated while imports boomed, taking an evergrowing slice of the home market.

The Tories have created an economic disaster. Yet they blindly, dogmatically hold on to their course. They call it the 'resolute approach'.

Jobs to the slaughter

There are now *3.2 million people officially out of work in the UK*—one in seven of the labour force, two million more than when the Tories came to office. The real jobs shortage is even worse than the official figures show. When those on special government schemes and those not claiming benefits are counted, five million people who want a job have not got one.

Even on the official figures, the scale of *long-term unemployment* is horrific. By October last year, 1.2 million people had been out of work for more than twelve months. For young people under twenty-five, long-term unemployment has risen from 74,000 to 312,000 in the space of just two years.

The number of people still in jobs has fallen dramatically. *Manufacturing employment* has plummeted 22 per cent since mid-1979. Jobs in metal manufacture have fallen 37 per cent; in coal and petroleum products, 35 per cent; textiles, 33 per cent; vehicles, 28 per cent; and mechanical engineering, 24 per cent.

Unemployment in Northern Ireland is over 20 per cent; in the North and Wales, it is more than 17 per cent. Traditionally prosperous regions are fast closing the gap. The number of jobless has risen most rapidly in the West Midlands—to over three times higher than when Labour left office. Many localities have been hit particularly hard: unemployment is around 30 per cent in Pembroke Dock, Tenby, Consett, Rothesay, Mablethorpe, Hunstanton, Ilfracombe; and nearly 40 per cent in Strabane and other places in Northern Ireland.

Young people under twenty-five make up 40 per cent of the jobless total. Two out of three school leavers cannot find work. 460,000 will enter the new Youth Training Scheme this year; half will go on the dole at the end.

Over 860,000 *women* are counted as unemployed. More than a million more would like to work, but are too discouraged to register as unemployed. 'Last in' during economic expansion, they're the 'first out' in recession.

One in six *black people* are out of work (1981 figures) compared with one in ten white people. This has been exacerbated by a significant increase in discrimination in white-collar jobs since the mid-1970s.

Jobs losses have hit hardest among the *low paid*. Over three-quarters of unemployed men were in jobs paying

Phil Evans.

below the national average. These workers haven't 'priced themselves out of jobs'.

The *waste* is enormous. Unemployment this year will cost *£17 billion* in lost tax revenues and increased benefit payments—almost £100 a week for each extra person out of work. The cost in lost production is even greater—up to £30 billion a year.

The *social cost* is incalculable. A Manpower Services Commission study of the long-term jobless in 1980 drew a disturbing picture of anxiety, depression, ill-health and financial hardship. Other studies, based on American experience, have found that for every 100,000 people who lose their jobs, deaths increase by 5,000, mental hospital admissions by 6,000 and prison intake by 1,900. A Department of Health research project reached similar conclusions, but its report was suppressed.

Band aids

The Tories pretend that mass unemployment is due to excessive wages rather than their own policies, and have designed special 'employment measures' accordingly:

● The *Young Workers Scheme* provides a £15 per week subsidy to employers for each young person they take on below £40 per week. Nine out of ten jobs covered would have existed anyway. Only 10,000 extra new jobs have been created. The cost: £6,000 a year each.

● The *Temporary Short-time Working Compensation Scheme* has been cut back in scope and in the level of pay—from 75 per cent to 50 per cent of normal pay.

● The *Community Programme* run by the Manpower Services Commission has been forced to cut wage rates for the long-term unemployed on temporary jobs.

● The *Small Firms' Employment Subsidy*, which created 82,000 extra jobs in its brief lifespan under the Labour government, has been abolished.

● The *Job Release Scheme*, set up by Labour to encourage older workers to retire early, has been restricted in scope: the qualifying age for males has been increased to sixty-four.

● The new *Job-Splitting Scheme* is intended to cut wages

and to take away employment protection rights from workers, not to create employment or more flexible work patterns.

The Tories have also slashed the public employment services, making the jobless more vulnerable. They have:

● Cut back the *Job Centre network* and threatened large parts of it with privatisation.

● Abolished the *Occupational Guidance Service* for young people.

● Abandoned a *computer-aided matching scheme* planned by the Labour government.

● Closed *Employment Rehabilitation Centres* with tragic results for the disabled, elderly workers, ex-offenders and the chronically sick.

Monetarism

'*Almost all the tenets of monetarism have been destroyed.*'

Sir Ian Gilmour MP, former Tory cabinet minister, in *Britain Can Work*, 1983

'*Monetarism is not a party political doctrine. If the supply of money exceeds the supply of goods and services there will be inflation.*'

Margaret Thatcher, 10 December 1981

This is Mickey Mouse economics. In 1982 the 'supply of money' was £90 billion. The 'supply of goods and services' was £270 billion. Yet we still had 8 per cent inflation.

How they said it should work...

'*The way to get the economy moving is to get inflation down.*'

...and how they were proved wrong

Inflation has eventually come down—after more than doubling in the Tories' first year. But the economy has gone into reverse—and there are no signs of any new jobs.

11

'The way to get inflation down is to hold down the money supply. After a lag of a year or two that will hold down prices.'

In fact the money supply grew at roughly *double* the government's target rates before stabilising in the last year. If prices followed money supply, inflation would now be soaring up to 20 per cent.

'The way to hold down the money supply is to cut the amount the public sector borrows.'

Academic studies have shown no link at all between public borrowing and money growth in the 1970s.

'The way to cut public borrowing is to cut public spending.'

Spending cuts throw people out of work. That cuts tax revenue and pushes up spending on benefits. **Result**: more public borrowing. The Tories have borrowed 25 per cent *more* than Labour in cash terms.

'The control of the money supply is really only a façade or a smokescreen. The important consequence of the Government's economic strategy is to alter the balance of bargaining power, to weaken the trade unions through the intensification of unemployment, and thereby to succeed in bringing wage settlements well below the rate of inflation; that is to say, to reduce real wages.'

Lord Kaldor, economist and Labour peer, speech in the House of Lords, 27 November 1980

Silent mills

After four years of Tory rule, British industry is a disaster area. Production has suffered the biggest collapse for sixty years. Companies are going bust at a record rate. Investment has been cut by a third.

Firms are closing plants and laying off workers every week. Once-thriving industrial cities like Coventry now have one in eight on the dole.

This is not policy, it's punishment. The Tories claim to have laid the foundations for a competitive industry. But: investment in new machines and technologies has collapsed; fewer skilled workers are being trained; less is now being spent on product research and development. Britain's industry is falling even further behind:

● Manufacturing is now producing *one-fifth* less than when the Tories took over—less than in any year since 1967. The fall in output in the last four years is 19 per cent. In the Great Depression of 1929-31 output fell by just 12 per cent.

● Within manufacturing, textiles and clothing have been cut by a third. Steel production has been slashed by half. In each of the last three years Britain has produced less steel than in the early 1950s.

● Output of cars is down by a quarter to the lowest level since 1957, and production of commercial vehicles in 1981 couldn't even match our output in 1950.

Under the hammer

● In 1982 there were over 12,000 company liquidations in England and Wales—more than two-and-a-half times as many as in 1979 and the highest level ever recorded.

● Personal bankruptcies are up—by 60 per cent since 1979.

● Auctions of machinery from closed-down factories have attracted buyers from all over the world. Bidders at Europe's largest-ever auction of used machinery at Talbot's car plant at Linwood, Scotland, in November 1981, included Swedish car makers Saab Scania and companies from Canada, the USA, India, Israel and South Africa.

Yesterday's people

Companies which closed down or went into receivership under the Tories. In some cases the receivers have been able to salvage parts of the company. Often the brand names have been taken over by other companies.

Airlines: Laker Airways, British Cargo Airlines
Carpets: Homfray Carpets, BMK, Forfar
              Carpets

Clothing makers:	Janet Reger (underwear), Morland (sheepskin wear), Libro (leisure wear), Lovable (bras), Alligator (rainwear), Nelbarden (swimwear)
Engineering:	Alfred Herbert (machine tools), Stone Platt (textile machinery), Aurora Holdings (Britain's last full-range special steel manufacturer), Carron's Iron Works, Wilson Watson Engineering, Fairbairn Lawson (foundry), Mallins
Financial Institutions:	Isle of Man Savings Bank, Norton Warburg (investment advisers), Hedderwick Stirling Grumbar (stockbrokers)
Football clubs:	Wolverhampton Wanderers, Hull City (rugby league), Blackpool (rugby league)
Furniture:	Austins, Liden, Jaycee, Harrison Lebus, Orthopaedic Bedding Co., New Age Kitchens
Household goods:	Aeonics (duvets), Royal Stafford China, Viners (cutlery), Ronson (lighters, etc)
Shoes:	Norvic, Mr Henry
Shops:	Jacksons of Piccadilly, Swan and Edgar, Bourne's, Timothy Whites, Dicky Dirts, Crocodile, Supasave, John Michael, Biba
Toymakers:	Airfix, Lesney, Berwick Timpo, Dunbee Combex Marx, Triang
Vehicle Makers:	De Lorean (sports cars), Foden (trucks), Hesketh (motorcycles), Bamfords (agricultural machinery), Caravans International, Westerley Marine (boats)
Others:	Oxley Printers, Fakenham Press, Alan Pond (garages), Lockwoods (canned foods), Atcost (farm buildings)

Sink or swim

The Tories' attitude to industry is—if it can't swim, let it sink. But just to be helpful the government is busily deflating the lifejackets offered by regional aid, sacking the swimming instructors of the National Enterprise Board, and piling the lead weights of monetarism onto industry's back. Public corporations in addition have one hand tied with tight financial limits. It's not surprising so much of industry has gone under.

The National Enterprise Board has been wound down. It was set up by the Labour government in 1975 to build high technology industries, to help small businesses and to put ailing firms back on their feet.

● First, the government moved the NEB's second largest subsidiary—Rolls Royce—out of its control and placed it under the Department of Industry. The entire board of the NEB, including chairperson Leslie Murphy, resigned in protest in November 1979.

● The government then moved in with new guidelines and a new Industry Act in June 1980 which changed the role of the board from 'extending public ownership into profitable areas' to 'promoting private ownership of interests'. The NEB was to sell off its profitable holdings in companies such as ICL, Fairey engineering and Ferranti.

● The next step—in July 1981—was to merge the NEB with the National Research and Development Corporation to form the British Technology Group. Public funds for the group have been cut back from £70 million in 1979/80 to only £10 million planned this year.

Despite Margaret Thatcher's election pledge to maintain 'a strong and effective regional policy', aid for the regions has suffered major cutbacks.

● In July 1979 Sir Keith Joseph redrew the regional aid map to cut the proportion of the working population in assisted areas from 43 per cent to 25 per cent.

● Regional aid has been cut by 44 per cent since Labour's last year.

● Regional development grants and finance for the Scottish and Welsh development agencies have been cut by over 25 per cent.

Future shock

Industry can survive in world markets only if it invests in the most efficient and up-to-date machines and technologies. That is just where Britain has been weak. Under the Tories, industry has become weaker still:

In 1978, £874 was invested in new machinery and factories for every worker in British manufacturing. In the same year: £1,419 per worker was invested in the USA; £1,558 in Germany; and £3,642 in Japan.

Since the Tories took over, investment in manufacturing industry has slumped by *one-third*, to the lowest level since 1959. Even including the assets that industry leases or rents rather than buys, investment has fallen by a quarter in the last four years, and was lower in 1982 than in 1961.

At the end of the 1970s research and development expenditure in relation to output in private manufacturing in Britain was half that of the major European industrialised countries, and second from the bottom amongst the top 25 western countries.

Output per worker in manufacturing is now only 5 per cent higher than when the Tories took over. In the previous four years it rose more than 14 per cent.

Trained for the dole

Britain lags behind most other industrial countries in industrial training. The Tories have made the situation worse by cutting back its statutory framework, claiming that individual employers left to themselves will do enough. They have:

Abolished 16 of the 23 Industrial Training Boards and allowed apprenticeships to fall to under half the level of the late 1960s.

Frustrated the Manpower Services Commission's 'New Training Initiative', which would have provided high-quality training throughout working life and a modernised system of apprenticeships.

Reduced the value of training allowances by 16 per cent and tried to make schemes compulsory.

Even suggested military service as a training option.

People are being trained not for work but for the dole. Towards the end of the year, 460,000 young people will enter the new Youth Training Scheme: less than half will have a job at the end.

'What if we are just left with ashes?'

'We shall in future see a real revival in our country's fortunes if we hold to the path we are now on. We are reaching the trough of the recession and it will start to turn up towards the end of next year.'

Margaret Thatcher, 28 November 1980

How long do we have to wait for the promised upturn?

'1981 will be the year when results begin to show.'

Margaret Thatcher, 4 January 1981

'There are now clear signs that the worst of the recession is over.'

Margaret Thatcher, 25 June 1981

Two years later, unemployment is still rising.
And will continue to rise. All forecasts paint a bleak picture: *unemployment* will go up at least to 1985. Adult unemployment will be higher in 1986 than it is now. *Inflation* will go up. *Manufacturing output* will grow slowly—but by 1986 will still be more than a tenth below what it was in 1979.

'There is much talk of industry rising like a phoenix from the ashes. But what if we are just left with ashes?'

Reg Parkes, former chairperson,
West Midlands CBI, 1980

'As I look round this region I see nothing but ashes.'

Reg Parkes, two years later

Collapse at home

British industry is in retreat.

● In 1982, for the first time ever, we imported more manufactured goods than we exported.

● Imports took 28.5 per cent of sales of all manufactures, up more than an eighth since 1979; 46 per cent of electrical engineering products (up a quarter), 46 per cent of vehicles (up more than a fifth), 41 per cent of textiles (up more than a quarter), 37 per cent of clothing and footwear (up more than a quarter).

True, there is a surplus on the current account of the Balance of Payments. It's there because:

● The economy's depressed, so we buy—and import —less than we would otherwise do.

● The pound is overvalued, so the same amount spent brings in more imports.

● North Sea oil plugged the gap. Without it, the £4 billion surplus of 1982 would have turned into an £8 billion deficit.

Collapse abroad

The Tories claim that the way to create jobs is to 'improve Britain's competitiveness in world markets'. In fact:

● According to the Bank of England's own measure of 'effective competitiveness', Britain's competitiveness *fell* by nearly 25 per cent in the Tories' first three years because

● our prices were rising much faster than those of overseas competitors.

● the government's high interest rate policy encouraged a big rise in the exchange rate—imports became cheap and British exports expensive.

● The pound has now come down, by 25 per cent from its peak. To restore competitiveness to its 1979 level would require a further fall of around 10 per cent.

Falling competitiveness has had a damaging impact on trade.

● The volume of Britain's exports—excluding oil—actually *fell* between 1978 and 1982. Exports of manufactured goods fell by over 3 per cent.

● Imports have soared under the Tories—by 21 per cent (excluding oil). Manufactured import volume has risen by a massive 31 per cent.

Away from it all

'Great international companies are demonstrating their faith in Britain's future by choosing this country under a

Conservative Government as the location for major expansion. This is the way to get thousands of extra jobs for Britain.'

Margaret Thatcher, Tory Party Conference, 1981

In November 1979, six months after taking office, the Tories dismantled exchange control. Money flooded out.

● Private investment overseas reached a massive £10,000 million in 1982—116 per cent more than in 1978.

● In the last four years a total of £35.4 billion has been invested overseas—more than double the £16.6 billion invested by people and companies abroad in the UK.

● Pension funds invested 26 per cent of their new funds overseas in 1982—compared to only 8 per cent in 1979.

● Total 'portfolio investment' overseas (shares and other securities) in the four years before 1979 came to £1,030 million. In the four years since, it has been £14,000 million.

The great private rip-off

The country's assets have been sold off at knockdown prices to help pay for tax concessions for the rich.

Already gone

Amersham International: all shares sold
British Aerospace: majority of shares sold
British National Oil Corporation: Britoil formed to take over BNOC's oil production, and majority of shares sold
British Petroleum: public stake reduced from 51 to 39 per cent
British Rail: some hotels and Seaspeed Hovercraft sold
British Steel: some subsidiaries, including Redpath Dorman Long, sold
British Transport Docks Board: renamed Associated British Ports and 49 per cent of shares sold
Cable and Wireless: half shares sold
Hydraulic Research Station: all shares sold
National Enterprise Board: some holdings, including ICL and Ferranti, sold
National Freight Corporation: sold to management

Planned to go

British Airways: shares and subsidiaries to be sold

British Gas Corporation: oil interests and showrooms to be sold

British Leyland: profitable subsidiaries could be sold

British Rail: shares in Sealink and other property to be sold

British Shipbuilders: shares to be sold

British Telecom: majority of shares to be sold

Central Electricity Generating Board: private generation of electricity in prospect

Computer Aided Design Centre: all shares to be sold

Forestry Commission: may be sold outright

National Bus Company: profitable parts to be sold

Post Office: joint public-private subsidiaries to be set up and then sold

Property Services Agency: contracting out to be introduced

Royal Ordnance Factories: to be put on a 'commercial footing'

Vehicle Testing Centres: may be sold to Lloyd's Insurance Brokers

Jobs lost in the nationalised industries:

British Steel: 82,300 (April 1979 to March 1983)

British Shipbuilders: 20,266 (April 1979 to April 1982)

British Airways: 20, 241 (April 1979 to April 1982)

British Rail: 32,198 (December 1978 to March 1983)

Central Electricity Generating Board: 6,226 (April 1979 to April 1982)

National Coal Board: 36,500 (December 1978 to March 1983)

Nigel Paige

Rich pickings for the City

● Tory tight money policies have helped the big four clearing banks to make record profits—£1,550 million a year on average in the last four years—more than *double* what they made in the previous four years. In 1981, profits were so high that even the Tories were prompted to introduce a once-off 'windfall profits tax'.

● The government has failed to supervise the City's markets, despite numerous scandals and growing evidence of shady dealings, particularly in the Lloyd's insurance market. The last two years have witnessed the collapse of investment advisers Norton Warburg and stockbrokers Hedderwick Stirling Grumbar. At Lloyd's five former directors of insurance brokers Alexander Howden were accused of misappropriating $55 million. Leading underwriter Ian 'Goldfinger' Posgate, reputedly the highest paid man in the City, was suspended by the Lloyd's council following allegations of irregularities. The chairperson of top brokers, Minet Holdings, was forced to resign when he admitted benefiting from reinsurance deals. Three directors of a Minet subsidiary were later dismissed.

● Merchant banks and stockbrokers have made fortunes out of the government's privatisation programme. Advice and professional services in connection with just four sell offs—British Aerospace, Cable and Wireless, National Freight Corporation and Amersham International—were worth £12 million in fees alone. Commission of 1.25 per cent on the value of the issue represented further gains.

● Privatisation has given speculators a field day. They apply for shares at the price set by the government, wait till the price soars in the days after the sale, and sell out quick. The Associated British Ports issue was oversubscribed 25 times and speculators made an immediate 20 per cent profit. First day profits of 36 per cent were made on Amersham International, 17 per cent on Cable and Wireless and 14 per cent on British Aerospace.

The worst record in the western world

Since the Tories took over, Britain has become self-sufficient in oil—an advantage shared only by Norway. Yet Britain has suffered:

● **The highest unemployment** of any industrial country apart from Spain.

● **The biggest increase in unemployment** in the industrialised world. More than 7 per cent of the workforce has been added to the dole queues.

● The biggest fall in industrial production in any major country apart from Canada. Since 1979, while Britain's industry slumped by over 11 per cent, the average fall in industrial countries was only 3 per cent.

● The biggest rise in prices in any major country apart from Italy, Spain and France. Under the Tories, prices have risen by over 50 per cent—compared to an average for the industrial countries of 40 per cent.

Norway is a similar oil-rich industrial country. In the last four years its industrial output has increased by 15 per cent. Unemployment is below 2.5 per cent.

John Minnion

Tory ups and downs

Up

Unemployment
from 1.219 million (May 1979) to 3.199 million (February 1982)—*up* 162 per cent.

Company liquidations
from 4,537 (1979) to 12,039 (1982)—*up* 165 per cent.

Prices +
from 216 (May 1979) to 326 (January 1983)—*up* 51 per cent.

Down

Employment
from 23.107 million (June 1979) to 20.974 million (September 1982)—*down* 9.2 per cent.

Output*
from 112.2 (second quarter 1979) to 107.6 (last quarter 1982)— *down* 4 per cent.

Industrial output* +
from 115.1 (second quarter 1979) to 100.9 (last quarter 1982)—*down* 12.3 per cent.

Manufacturing Output* +
from 107.4 (second quarter 1979) to 86.9 (last quarter 1982)—*down* 19.1 per cent

Manufacturing investment
(1975 prices) £987 million (second quarter 1979) to £636 million (last quarter 1982)—*down* 35.6 per cent.

Living standards +
from 112.0 (second quarter 1979) to 109.0 (third quarter 1982)—*down* 2.7 per cent.

* seasonally adjusted
+ index (1975 = 100)

Rich and poor

In Tory Britain rich and poor are moving further apart. All but the wealthiest have been made worse-off in the last four years.

● Living standards have been cut by rising prices and rising taxes while pay and benefits have been held down. In 1981 we suffered the biggest fall in a single year since the war.

● Pay has been held down by the Tories' secret incomes policy—mass unemployment.

● The tax burden overall has increased to make the Tories the highest taxing government ever in Britain.

● Inequality in income and wealth has been made worse by tax handouts to the rich.

● Meanwhile, millions more are forced onto the margins of poverty, beaten down by cuts in the value of benefits.

The slump in standards

Most people are worse-off under the Tories. Living standards, measured by 'real personal disposable income', are now more than 2 per cent lower than in the first half of 1979. After peaking at the end of 1980, they have fallen sharply—by nearly 6 per cent. The fall in 1981—2.1 per cent —was the biggest in a single year since the war.

Britain has fallen even further behind other countries. In 1978, our standard of living was 90 per cent of the average of the industrial countries. By 1981, it had fallen to 85 per cent. The reasons are simple:

● Pay, for those in work, has gone up by 59 per cent. But most of this has been eaten away by the increase in prices—51 per cent.

● That leaves a small increase in gross pay, but **take-home pay** has been cut by increases in national insurance contributions costing an average of nearly £5 a week.

● If those still in work are marginally better-off, the big increase in unemployment has meant a big drop in income for many.

> • Benefits have been squeezed for most groups who rely on them.
>
> The fall in living standards has been greatest for the unemployed, for people in council housing, and for workers in depressed manufacturing industries.

The boom in prices

The Tories sent inflation soaring in their first year, more than doubling the rate from 10 to 22 per cent. The increase in VAT added nearly 4 per cent to prices. Prices of nationalised industries were forced up—more than 86 per cent compared with 51 per cent for prices overall. Rents, rates and interest rates were all hiked. And one of the Tories' first measures was to abolish the *Price Commission* which, under Labour, checked prices.

Since peaking in 1980 inflation has dropped to around 5 per cent—largely because the economy is flat on its back. But the 13 per cent average rate of inflation under the Tories is *higher* than the 10 per cent rate they inherited from Labour.

Prices then...	...and now[1]	
prescription	20p	£1.40
visit to optician[2]	£6.15	£15.50
visit to dentist[3]	£5.00	£13.50
council rent (average)	£6.40	£14.45
school meal	25p	50p
minimum fare on London Underground	10p	40p
day return from London to Birmingham	£7.70	£12.00
gas (per therm)	15.3p	33.5p
electricity (per KWH)	3.07p	5.095p
20 cigarettes	57p	£1.09
pint of beer	40p	61p
first-class letter	10p	16p
second-class letter	8p	12.5p
telephone call[4]	6p	8.6p
pint of milk	13.5p	21p

1. 'then' = May 1979; 'now' = April 1983.   2. Maximum charge for lenses.
3. Maximum charge for routine treatment.   4. Three-minute local call, peak period.

The squeeze on pay

The Tories are using mass unemployment backed by anti-union legislation to force down living standards and promote inequality.

Real pay has grown very slowly—by just 5 per cent in four years. But not for everyone. Workers in steel and ship-building have taken a real cut of 9 per cent; in textiles, 3 per cent; and in mechanical engineering, 1 per cent. In the public sector workers have had to wrestle with cash limits, ceilings imposed by government on central spending, grants to councils and borrowing by nationalised industries, which each year have aimed to keep wage increases below the rise in the cost of living.

The extent of low pay is vast. Almost a third of the full-time adult workforce—1.9 million men and 2.4 million women—received less than two-thirds the average wage last year. A further three million part-time workers were also low paid. Measures taken by the government to squeeze pay include:

● Repeal of Schedule 11 of the Employment Protection Act, which gave workers a right to arbitration and fair wages.

● Abolition of the Clegg Comparability Commission, which compared pay in the public services and the private sector.

● Scrapping of the Pay Research Unit, which compared civil servants' pay with pay in the private sector.

● Repeal of the Fair Wages Resolution, which guaranteed fair wages for those employed under government contracts.

● Refusal to amend adequately the Equal Pay Act to ensure equal pay for work of equal value.

The Tories are determined to remove all statutory support for collective bargaining, all sources of strength for workers in negotiations with employers. Even their special job schemes (page 10) are designed to reinforce low pay.

● In 1979, less than one in ten *male manual workers* were receiving low wages—by 1981, the proportion was almost one in six.

● In 1979, two out of every three *women manual workers*

were low paid—by 1981, the proportion was three out of four.

Publicly, the Tories claim that British workers are overpaid. In private, they sing a different tune:

'Most of our competitors have much higher labour costs. The provisional figures for 1979 for the cost of employing someone, on the average wage, including social security taxes etc., are United States £7,200 p.a., West Germany £9,000 p.a., United Kingdom £5,000 p.a.'
Nicholas Ridley, now a Treasury Minister, speaking to a local Conservative association, 1 July 1980

Piling on the tax

The Tories promised to cut taxes. In fact they have systematically *increased* taxes for all but the rich. The overall tax burden on a worker on average earnings has gone up from 44 per cent of income in Labour's last year to 48 per cent today, even *after* the tax cuts in this year's budget. This has been done by:

● Virtually doubling the VAT rate from 8 per cent to 15 per cent in 1979.

● Increasing national insurance contributions in three steps from 6.5 per cent to 9 per cent (and from 4 per cent to 6.85 per cent for workers in pension schemes outside the state earnings-related scheme).

● Increasing the 25 per cent tax rate on the first £750 of taxable income to 30 per cent.

● Forcing up rates by cutting grants to local councils.

Income tax has been cut a little. The basic rate came down 3 points to 30 per cent in 1979, and personal allowances have been increased 5 per cent faster than prices over the last four years. But the income level at which a couple start paying income tax is lower—even after the Budget increase in allowances—than in any EEC country except Italy and Denmark.

Win or lose here's Howe

A typical company director on £45,000 a year has enjoyed a £120 a week rise in real take-home pay under Howe, an in-

27

crease of a quarter.

By contrast, a typical worker is worse-off by £15.30 a week, a cut of 21.3 per cent.

Institute of Fiscal Studies, March 1983

Polarising incomes

Incomes in Britain are unevenly spread: the top tenth of earners get 27 per cent of personal income before tax (24 per cent after tax) and the bottom half 23 per cent (26 per cent).

Tory tax measures have made the distribution of income more unequal.

They taxed the poor more, and the rich less. The rich gain from:

● The **3 per cent reduction of the basic rate** in 1979. At 1983 prices, this was worth £6.50 a week to a higher rate taxpayer, £3 a week to the average earner, and nothing at all to a taxpayer on £75 a week.

● **Concessions on higher rates of tax and the investment income surcharge (IIS).** The top tax rate has been cut from 83 per cent to 60 per cent, for earned income, and from 98 per cent to 75 per cent on investment income. The threshold for IIS has been raised from £1,700 to £7,100, an increase of nearly 150 per cent in real terms.

● **A range of tax concessions for small businesses**, which open new tax loopholes for higher-income earners.

Polarising wealth

Wealth is even more unevenly spread than income. The richest 1 per cent of Britain's adult population own as much as 23 per cent of all personal wealth. The richest 10 per cent own no less than 58 per cent of personal wealth, while the poorest 50 per cent share only 6 per cent. Under the Tories the rich get richer.

The Tories have neutered the *capital transfer tax* (CTT) which Labour established in 1975. They have:

● Limited the totting up of gifts to a ten-year period instead of the donor's whole lifetime.

● Doubled the CTT threshold from £25,000 to £50,000.

● Reduced the top rate on lifetime gifts from 75 per cent to 50 per cent.

- Allowed CTT tax bills to be paid in interest-free instalments.
- Extended the relief for agricultural land—previously restricted to owner-occupied farms—to tenanted land owned by absentee landlords.

The Tories have also introduced a major new concession in *capital gains tax* (CGT): from April 1982, all taxable gains will be reduced by a new allowance for inflation.

More on the bread line

In 1979 there were **eleven million people—one in five of the population—living in or on the margins of poverty:**

- Nearly four million people on supplementary benefits (the 'official' poverty line).
- Over two million *below* this poverty line.
- About five million people on incomes within 40 per cent of supplementary benefit levels.

Since then, the rise in unemployment and cuts in national insurance benefits put 2.5 million more people on to the poverty line—in May 1982 there were 6.5 million people living on supplementary benefit. In November 1979:

- There were 566,000 unemployed people claiming supplementary benefit. By December 1981 this had risen to 1,318,000.
- There were 306,000 single parents claiming supplementary benefit. By December 1981 this had risen to 369,000.
- There were 923,000 children in families living on supplementary benefit. By December 1981 there were 1.5 million children and today there are about 1.75 million.

On supplementary benefit an unemployed couple with two young children receive just £59.20 a week, plus rent and rates; a pensioner couple will get £52.30, plus rent and rates. All the needs of a child under eleven have to be met from £1.25 a day; and those of children aged between eleven and fifteen from £1.88 a day.

- In November 1980, the Tories restructured the supplementary benefit system—1.75 million claimants were made worse-off.

● In November 1982, the government introduced 'The Rossi Price Index': supplementary benefit rates were increased 0.5 per cent *less* than the estimated increase in the general Retail Price Index.

● From April 1983, supplementary benefit claimants have had their rent and rates met through a new scheme administered by local authorities. Two million people are worse-off by as much as 75p a week.

The 1979 Conservative manifesto said a Tory government would 'reduce the poverty trap', whereby taxes increase and benefit shrink with every pay rise. But:

● The number of families caught in the poverty trap has doubled since 1978—to 130,000—and the trap now extends over a wider range of incomes.

● Four out of five families who are poor enough to be claiming family income supplement are now paying tax.

Don't call me

The number of telephones disconnected due to nonpayment of telephone bills has increased by over 60 per cent since 1979—around 147,000 disconnections in 1979 compared with around 237,000 in 1982.

Telephone terminations are also believed to have risen —from around 33,000 in 1979 to an estimated 60,000 in 1982.

Onto the streets

In the first three years of Thatcher's government, court orders for recovery of rents rose by 847 per cent to 2,253, evictions rose by 19 per cent to 19,072 and residential property possession orders rose by 26 per cent to 88,000 (1981 figures).

Civil Judicial Statistics

Social insecurity

Because unemployment is higher, the Tories spend more on social security, but they pay less in benefits to each claimant. Thatcher's government is the first to have cut benefits since the 1930s:

Unemployment benefit was cut by 5 per cent in real terms and is now worth less than in 1979. It is at its lowest level relative to earnings since 1948.

The cut was 'justified' on the grounds that unemployment benefit escaped tax. In July 1982 the Tories made the benefit taxable but did *not* restore the 5 per cent cut and will not do so until November 1983—sixteen months later. Tax rebates are now withheld until a return to work or the end of the tax year.

Child additions to unemployment benefit have been cut—from £1.70 in November 1979 to just 30p a week in November 1982. Nearly 1.5 million children live in families where the head of the household is unemployed.

The *earnings-related* supplement to unemployment benefit was abolished from January 1982. It would now have been worth £18.60 a week to someone on average earnings.

As a result, a married man with two children on average earnings who becomes unemployed now will receive £38.45 a week less than he would have under the last Labour government. That is a cut in income of 41 per cent. The unemployed are increasingly having to rely upon means-tested supplementary benefit. Over two-thirds of the unemployed are now receiving supplementary benefit.

● *Child benefit* is worth 25p less than in April 1979 and the 1983 increase will do no more than restore the Tory cuts.

● Since March 1982, most new mothers receive child benefit monthly—a strain on the weekly budget.

● A pensioner couple have lost £2.25 a week (single persons £1.45) because the Tories broke the link between *pensions* and earnings.

● This year's pension increase, at 2 per cent below the rate of inflation, will cost a married couple £1 a week.

● The £57 ceiling on permitted earnings is lower in real terms than in 1978-9. The Tories promised to 'phase-out the "earnings rule" during this parliament'.

● National insurance *sickness benefit* has been abolished in the first eight weeks of sickness. Employers are now responsible for statutory sick pay. No account is taken of family responsibilities; the low paid are penalised.

● Industrial injury benefit has been abolished.

● Invalidity benefit was cut by 5 per cent, the link with earnings snapped. A married invalidity pensioner has lost £4.25 a week under the Tories.

Grabbed from the poor

Government savings in 1982-3 as a result of:

	£ million
Breaking the link between pensions and earnings	500
Deferring the 1980 benefit increase by two weeks	100
Abolishing the earnings-related supplement and cutting several benefits by 5 per cent in 1980	500
Recovering 1 per cent 'overshoot' on benefits in 1981	200
Introducing statutory sick pay scheme (in 1983-4)	400
Cutting child additions to national insurance benefit	50
Cutting child benefit and paying it monthly	250
Increasing supplementary benefit by less than the Retail Price Index	30
Total	**2,030**

and given to the rich

The cost in 1982-3 of Tory tax concessions to the rich:

Changes in income tax 1979 and 1983	1,440
Changes in investment income surcharge 1979 and 1983	320
Business start-up schemes, etc., 1981, 1982 and 1983	150
Retirement annuity relief 1980 and 1982	105
Capital transfer tax 1980, 1981 and 1983	180
Capital gains tax 1980, 1981, 1982 and 1983	315
Total	**2,405**

Value then...   ...and now

	May 1979	*in 1983 prices*
Child benefit	£6.10	£ 5.85[1]
Unemployment benefit	£25.40	£25.00
Pension (single person)	£34.30[2]	£32.85
Pension (couple)	£54.80[2]	£52.55

---

1. Child benefit is rising to £6.50 in November 1983. It would have been £6.54 if Labour's proposed 1979 uprating had been carried through and its real value maintained. Labour would have raised it to £7.85 this year.
2. What the pension would have been worth today if the link with earnings had not been broken.

Frauds big and small

The government claims to have 'saved' £271 million in 1981-2 throught its efforts in combatting social security fraud. By contrast, the Inland Revenue claims £4,000 million a year tax is being lost.

During the first year in office the government put an extra 1,050 people in the DHSS on tracing 'social security scroungers'. The following year, it added another 150 at the DHSS and 30 at Department of Employment offices.

In the first two years of this government staff at the Inland Revenue was *cut* by 11,500 to 73,500. Since then, the Inland Revenue has agreed to deploy an extra 100 people to cut down on tax dodges by the self-employed and 300 to check for tax evasion by people with second jobs.

Nigel Paige

Free-fire zone in the public services

Cut, dismember, amputate

Cuts in public spending are at the core of Tory economic and monetary strategy. They cut when they can—capital spending in almost all services is a prime target. Where, as a consequence of their own policies, they can't cut, they do everything to limit increases—as in social security spending, where more money is spent on unemployment because there is more of it, but less on each unemployed person.

Public spending has been cut by £11,500 million compared with Labour's last plans. Spending as a proportion of total national income has in fact increased—but that is because income itself has dropped.

More spending doesn't mean higher standards. It often obscures worse treatment but for more clients, as in the case of the jobless or pensioners. The Tories have not been altogether successful in cutting local government spending, for there they face strong opposition from Labour-controlled authorities and foot-dragging compliance from their own supporters. But they have been effective in cutting local government jobs, by 110,000 since 1979, or 5 per cent. And they have cut the central government civil service by 80,000 or 11 per cent.

Drought at the parish pump

The Tories have squeezed spending by local councils by:

● Cuts in government grants through the Rate Support Grant system (RSG).

● Setting new spending limits.

● Penalising councils that spend above the limit by withdrawing grants.

● Limiting councils' ability to plan building programmes.

The result since May 1979 has been:

● A 3.5 per cent cut in the real value of current spending by councils.

● More than 40 per cent cuts in spending on building and repairing houses, schools, roads, old people's homes and other vital services.

● A massive £1.5 billion underspend on building works in 1982-3.

The Tories have tried to blame the councils:

● For trying to protect services by putting up rates —which have almost doubled since May 1979.

● For not spending all the building money allocated to them.

To reinforce the cuts the Tories have attacked councillors' rights to manage council finances. They have:

● Banned mid-year rate increases in England and Wales.

● Taken away the right to use revenue money for capital spending above government allocations.

In their enthusiasm to curb local services the Tories have:

● Gone outside the law. Penalties imposed on English and Welsh councils in 1980 were declared unlawful by the courts.

● Made a mess of their own proposals. Legislation has been proposed, withdrawn, redrafted, withdrawn again.

They have:

● Revised criteria for penalties in a blatantly political way, to try to avoid their application to Tory councils.

Schooling

'We must restore to every child, regardless of background, the chance to progress as his or her abilities allow.'
Conservative manifesto, 1979

'I think I am presiding at the moment over an education system in which there really is inadequate provision for a very substantial minority.'
Sir Keith Joseph, Secretary of State for Education,
20 February 1983

The Tories are dismantling the principles of state education set up in 1944 and promoting the private sector. Women who protest about cuts in nursery provision are told that a woman's place is in the home. Parents who complain about falling standards and essential school books are told to buy the books themselves—or to apply for an assisted place at a private school. Pupils who cannot afford school meals are told to bring sandwiches. Young people who are denied entry to higher education are told that such education is now no longer a right but a privilege.

The Tories have cut education spending by 6 per cent in real terms.

Nursery education

Under the Tories, the three- and four-year-olds' contingent in full-time education in nursery schools increased by a mere 4 per cent between 1979 and 1981, and then fell by 5.4 per cent between 1981 and 1982. This compares with a 26.5 per cent increase between 1976 and 1979. There are even fewer children attending full-time nursery classes in primary schools. Current plans are to cut the proportion of three-and four-year-olds receiving full-time and part-time education of all sorts from 40 per cent in 1981-2 to 35 per cent in 1984-5.

The chance of securing a nursery place for a child depends almost wholly on where he or she lives: under Labour, Walsall provided 91 per cent of three- and four-year-olds with nursery education; in Tory West Sussex, 10 per cent receive it.

Conservative-controlled Local Education Authorities (LEAs) have been cutting provisions. Some LEAs, such as Oxfordshire, actually proposed to close *all* their nursery schools. When it became apparent that LEAs have a statutory duty to provide nursery education and could not cancel it, the Tories introduced legislation which removed that duty.

Schools

582 state schools, including 135 secondary schools, were approved for closure by the Thatcher government in the three years 1980-2. Falling school rolls are not the only factor. Government cuts are a major cause.

Spending cuts are also having a serious effect on standards in schools. In 1980, the government Inspectorate found four LEAs in breach of their minimum statutory duties as set out in the 1944 Education Act. In 1981, the inspectors reported a reduction in levels of provision in 71 LEAs (almost three-quarters) compared with 1980 and an ever-widening gap in provision between LEAs.

● In 1981 in England, government cuts forced almost a third of local education authorities to increase the number of mixed age classes in primary schools and a reduction in small teaching groups for remedial work in just over a tenth.

● One in six primary schools now have officially unsatisfactory teaching provision. 1.07 million primary school children are in single-teacher classes of over 30 and 132,000 are in single-teacher classes of over 35.

● A quarter of primary schools and a third of secondary schools have officially unsatisfactory book provisions. Between 1978-9 and 1981-2, spending on books fell from £12.20 to £11.40 per primary pupil and from £22.70 to £19.90 per secondary pupil.

● An estimated 500,000 pupils in primary schools in England and a third of a million secondary school pupils suffered a worsening of pupil-teacher ratios between 1980 and 1981. Average sixth form class sizes have increased by 9 per cent since 1979. There have been no significant improvements in the pupil-teacher ratios overall, despite a fall of about one million in the school population since 1979.

● About one-fifth of secondary schools lack appropriately qualified staff: one in five maths teachers in secondary schools is not qualified.

● The HMI's report a reduction in the range of courses. Courses such as child care, motor vehicle technology and remedial education, and out-of-school activities are being dropped.

● Music and physical education is also being cut. Many Tory LEA began charging for instrumental music lessons until it was found to be unlawful—now they have just abandoned them. Sir Keith Joseph has been forced to admit that 'we fail to provide many pupils with a broad, balanced, coherent curriculum'.

● One in three school science laboratories is inadequately equipped.

● School premises are deteriorating. A quarter of primary schools and about a third of secondary schools are in urgent need of repair or decoration.

● 18,000 teaching posts have been axed by the Tories. A further 20,000 are to go by 1983-4. Over 26,000 teachers were registered as unemployed in September 1982, and one in five newly-qualified teachers were unable to obtain a post—all due to the cuts.

Comprehensives
Ninety per cent of local authority pupils attend comprehensive schools, but fully comprehensive education is a long way away. Many so-called comprehensive schools are in the catchment area of a grammar or a private school: many able pupils are creamed off. The Tories' Education Act 1979 allows local authorities to keep the unfair eleven plus. Tory Kingston-upon-Thames has not one comprehensive school.

Education vouchers
The Tories are intent on putting education in the market place. Their proposed education vouchers will do nothing to improve educational standards. They will enhance private education and will destroy comprehensive education. A two-tier system will be established: popular schools in leafy suburbs will become overcrowded and inner city schools will be forced either to close or to decline into 'sink schools'—secondary moderns in all but name.

Private schools
Private schools are a major obstacle to a completely free education system. They transfer economic status, social position and influence from generation to generation. Encouraged by the Tories, they harm the maintained sector by poaching many academic pupils from comprehensive schools. The Tories' Assisted Places Scheme used £12.4 million of tax payers' money to buy places for 8,600 pupils in private schools in 1982-3.

Special education
The Warnock Report proposed the integration of most pupils with special needs (e.g. physically or mentally han-

dicapped) within ordinary schools. But the government has refused to provide any extra cash to implement the proposals contained in its Education Act 1981. According to the National Union of Teachers, one in ten local education authorities is breaking the law by failing to provide full-time study for the handicapped up to the age of nineteen.

School meals
The Tories are dismantling the school meals service. The price of school meals was fixed at 25p in early 1979. It is now uncontrolled and averages 50p. They have allowed Tory local authorities such as Merton to abolish all school meals for pupils with the exception of handicapped pupils and a few poor pupils still entitled to free meals. Paid school meals have dropped from 64 per cent of the total in 1978, to 49 per cent in 1981. Some Tory local authorities are even planning to privatise the school meals service.

Education after eighteen
The Tories have cut training opportunities for young workers and reduced the few grants for 16-year-olds continuing in full-time-education (see section on Young People).

This Tory government has been the first government to abandon the 1963 Robbins' principle that higher education should be available to all who have the ability to pursue it. Places at universities will be reduced by about one in six by next year, despite an increase in the eighteen-year-old population.

Of Britain's forty-four *universities*, fourteen are facing financial cuts of over 20 per cent. The worst hit are Salford (up to 44 per cent cut); Keele (33 per cent); Bradford (33 per cent); and Aston (31 per cent). Many of these universities are renowned for their technological work and for their contribution to industrial innovation. Many important research projects are being abandoned. About 4,000 teaching jobs in higher education have been lost since 1979. Since 1980, there has been an estimated 6 per cent deterioration in university staff-student ratios.

Cuts in *polytechnics* and *colleges of higher education* continue; the government has asked its National Advisory Body to cut courses in the sector, by 10 per cent. Most *overseas students* are now charged full-cost fees which have drastically increased by 300 per cent since 1979, e.g. 300 per cent for arts undergraduates.

Student grants have fallen by 10 per cent in real terms over the same period. So much for the Tory Party's election manifesto which stated that 'much of our higher education in Britain has a world-wide reputation for its quality' and which pledged 'to ensure that this excellence is maintained'.

The government is seriously considering the introduction of *student loans*. Half the money now available to students in the form of grants would be replaced by a government loan and the rest would be given as a grant, with *students repaying the loan* on taking up employment. A loan scheme restricts access to post-school education. It discourages students from low-income families which cannot afford loan repayments.

The Tories are damaging *adult* and *continuing education*. Their insistence on 'self-financing' has resulted in

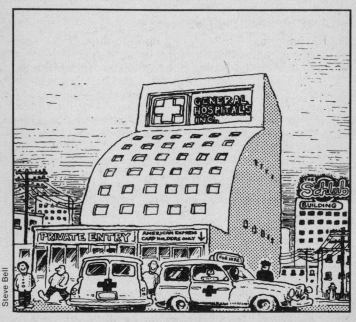

Steve Bell

evening-class fees shooting up and VAT has even been charged on some classes. Open University fees have gone up 79 per cent since 1981; and the number enrolling in adult education classes has gone down—from 2 to 1.38 million. Worse is to come. Spending is planned to fall from £81 million in 1982-3 to £65 million in 1983-4.

Health as privilege

The Tories have not made actual cuts in health service expenditure. But they have consistently undermined the basic principles of the National Health Service (NHS)—a service free at the point of use and funded out of general taxation—and its ability to provide good quality, comprehensive care and treatment for all. Resources have not increased sufficiently to allow for real growth; health charges have increased astronomically; certain services are to be 'privatised'; and private practice has been given every encouragement. The Tories are aiming at a two-tier health service, where the private sector will cater for the wealthy and healthy and an inadequate and demoralised NHS will cater for the rest.

Resources

The government claims that by 1984 it will have increased NHS resources by 7.5 per cent in real terms. In reality, health authorities have had their budgets squeezed. Some health authorities have received less than they need to maintain services.

● The growing number of very elderly people increases demand on the NHS. A person over seventy-five costs the health service nearly eight times the cost of someone of working age. The government calculates that 0.7 per cent growth a year is required to meet these demands.

● New medical techniques increase costs. The DHSS calculates 0.5 per cent growth a year is needed to accommodate this.

● Part of this 'growth' has had to come from 'efficiency savings'. The DHSS admits that only half of the £30 million savings called for in 1981 were achieved by more efficient use of resources. The rest came from cutting back on maintenance and deferring new projects at the expense of the long-term interests of the service.

● In 1982 regional health authorities had to find £65 million out of existing budgets to fund the government's revised pay offer to the health workers. They will have to do the same again this year.

● The additional resources have not matched the increase in demand for the NHS's services. The National Association of Health Authorities considers that an extra £160 million has been necessary just to keep up with demand in 1982 and 1983. Only £30 million more was made available.

● Resources are not distributed evenly across the country. Losses in some regions will be particularly large.

● In March 1982, there were 941 unused beds in hospitals in England because of lack of money. In November 1982, the DHSS told regional health authorities not to proceed with new hospital developments unless they had the revenue to run them. Information from eleven of the fourteen RHAs in December 1982 revealed that fifty-seven hospital schemes were under threat as a result, and many still are.

● A senior paediatrician estimated that, in 1983, 6,000 babies are likely to be deprived of the intensive care they need because of a shortage of facilities resulting from the cash squeeze.

● Savings of £170 million could be made on the NHS's £1.7 billion drug bills if generic substitutes were used; £29 million from replacing the eleven most popular branded drugs. But the government prefers to come to an arrangement with the drug companies to reduce profits, by around £24 million.

Charges

The Tories have penalised the sick by increasing health charges. The NHS is supposed to be a service 'free at the point of use'. But:

● Between May 1979 and April 1983 prescription charges rose from 20p to £1.40—an increase of 600 per cent.

● Between May 1979 and April 1983, the maximum charge

for routine dental treatment rose from £5 to £13.50—an increase of 170 per cent. Charges for more complicated treatment rose from £30 to £95—an increase of 217 per cent. In this, the government has ignored the advice of its own Dental Review Body.

● Optical charges have also been increased and the structure changed. Under Labour the charge for lenses ranged from £2.90 to £6.15. From April 1983, charges for single-vision lenses will range from £4 to £8.95, and charges for more complicated lenses from £9.20 to £15.50.

● In 1978-9 charges met 6.5 per cent of the cost of family practitioner services. This year they are expected to meet 11.5 per cent of the costs. Prescription, dental and optical charges will raise £340 million.

● In October 1982, the government introduced a new charge. Overseas visitors not covered by a reciprocal health agreement are required to pay for a stay in hospital. The government claimed it would raise £6 million a year, but took no account of the extra administrative costs involved. Reports of the new charges' implementation suggest that very little will be collected other than a further increase in racial tension.

Cancer research pinched

Government financial cutbacks in the universities have been a major factor in reducing the rate of expansion in cancer research. Many existing cancer research projects have been forced more on charities, which have therefore been able to finance fewer new projects. Since 1979 an estimated 50 cancer research projects which would normally have been funded by cancer charities have been refused assistance. Since 1979 extra demands on the Cancer Research Campaign's funds have led to a 60 per cent increase in the number of funding applications being refused.

Private practice

The Tories have actively encouraged the development of private practice. In 1980, Gerard Vaughan, then Minister for Health, suggested that 25 per cent of the country's health-care needs could be met by the private sector.

● They scrapped Labour's Health Service Board which supervised the removal of pay beds from the NHS. Between 1976 and 1980, the number of pay beds was reduced from 4,444 to 2,533. In the following two years, an additional 190 pay beds were made available in England. Controls on the development of private hospitals outside the NHS have also been relaxed. Only developments of 120 beds or more require the authority of the Secretary of State, as against 75 (or 100 in Greater London) under Labour.

● By June 1981, the number of beds in the private sector had risen from 29,819 to 32,380. In February 1982, Gerard Vaughan said he had been notified of 39 proposed new private developments since August 1980 which would provide a further 2,043 beds.

● They have encouraged the intrusion of the private sector into the public health service. They have lifted the ban on contractual arrangements between the NHS and profit-making hospitals and amended procedures regulating the disposal of surplus NHS land to allow private development.

● From April 1982, they gave tax relief on employers' contributions to private health insurance for employees earning £8,500 or less. The cost: £4 million in 1982-3.

● From January 1980, the government renegotiated the consultant's contract. All consultants can now undertake some private practice without losing any of their NHS salary.

● The number of subscribers to private health insurance has virtually doubled in the past four years, to over two million. The government is offering private health insurance to its 652,000 civil servants at specially discounted rates.

Privatisation

The government is undermining the NHS by requiring health authorities to put their catering, cleaning and laundry services out to competitive tender. Health authorities are to be allowed to reclaim VAT on services carried out by private companies. But:

'Private services are almost a third more expensive than the average of direct labour elsewhere in the authority.'
Oxford Area Health Authority, September 1981

'*Experience of outside contractors has shown that significant costs are incurred in supervising standards of the contract.*'

Sheffield Area Health Authority, October 1981

It is very doubtful that any savings made would exceed the £24 million the government will forgo through its VAT concession.

NHS staff

Not only are the Tories threatening the NHS's ability to provide good services—they now require those who work in it to subsidise it.

● The NHS is the country's biggest employer, employing about one million people. In 1982, 40 per cent of them earned *less* than the government's 'poverty line'.

● Over the Tories' first two years, health workers' wages were drastically reduced, both in real terms and relative to other public sector workers. In 1980, nurses accepted a 13 per cent rise when inflation was 18 per cent; in 1981, they were awarded 6 per cent when prices had risen 12 per cent. The 1982 pay settlement forced upon the health workers will mean a further reduction in their standard of living.

Inequality in health

The NHS has achieved much over the past thirty-five years. But major inequalities still exist in health standards:

● The Black Report of 1980 revealed that babies born to unskilled manual parents are *twice as likely to die at birth* or in the first month of life as babies born to parents from the professional classes. The sons of unskilled manual parents are five times, and daughters four times, as likely

Steve Bell

IF....
PARTY
POLITICAL
BROADCASTS
WERE
LEGAL
DECENT
HONEST ✓

THERE NOW FOLLOWS A PARTY POLITICAL BROADCAST ON BEHALF OF THE CONSERVATIVE PARTY.

"MY VOICE WILL PROBABLY BE MAKING SOME OF YOU FEEL RATHER ILL...

....IN FUTURE, THAT FEELING IS GOING TO COST YOU A GREAT DEAL OF MONEY...."

~Steve Bell~

to die in the following eleven months as children of professional-class parents. These inequalities are reflected throughout life and for most kinds of disease. For every man from the professional classes who dies from a respiratory disease, six unskilled manual workers die.

● The government published the report during the parliamentary recess. Initially, only 260 copies were printed and no press conference was given. Patrick Jenkin, then Secretary of State, refused to endorse the committee's recommendations and said the additional expenditure required to implement them was 'quite unrealistic in the present or any foreseeable economic circumstances'. It was not until the Labour opposition forced a debate in December 1982 that parliament even discussed the report.

● The government has taken much the same attitude towards evidence linking ill-health with unemployment. Dr Leonard Fagin's report on the subject was suppressed for five months before Labour MPs forced publication. Then only a small number of copies were printed at £6 each.

Re-organisation

The Tories reorganised the NHS as from April 1982, introducing cumbersome bureaucratic structures, and doing away with many of the democratic features introduced by the last Labour government.

● They reduced local authority representation on health bodies, from one-third to one-quarter.

● They cut representation of health service workers and encouraged health authorities to look for nominations from non-TUC affiliated unions.

● They have threatened the future of community health councils. In 1980 the government queried whether their existence was necessary after reorganisation. In 1981, it relented and said CHCs would be retained for the time being. But they have been cut in size and the government has withdrawn its funding of *CHC News*.

● The government is planning to make family practitioner committees independent health authorities in their own right. This will split the administration of important primary-care services between two authorities—and make effective planning of these services more difficult.

Getting nowhere on public transport

'On your bike' was Norman Tebbit's advice to the jobless. Why just them? After the Tory attack on transport, we all need to bike. Fares are up, services cut, railways starved of funds, which means more traffic jams on the roads. Instead of building a modern, efficient transport network, the government is allowing the system we have to fall apart.

British Rail

British Rail fares are 67 per cent higher than in 1979, much more than the rise in prices generally.

Total passenger miles in 1982 were 13 per cent down in 1979, and freight traffic fell.

Investment in 1982 was over £200 million less in real terms than in 1979. A deterioration in services is inevitable.

Some services are being cutback, and journey times lengthened. British Rail has warned that, unless more money is made available, 3,000 miles of track will have to be closed by 1990 along with a big reduction in locomotive availability and an increase in signalling failures.

● Electrification is being held up despite a joint Department of Transport-British Rail report which concluded that substantial benefits and a healthy financial rate of return would ensue.

● The rail network is under threat. The Serpell Report, commissioned by the government, has paved the way. Its terms of reference concentrated on financial objectives and ignored the needs of the travelling public. Its proposals would mean higher fares, poorer services, lost jobs, reduced maintenance. There's even a suggestion of lower safety standards. Some of the 'options' would isolate vast areas of the country.

Bus transport

Local authority revenue support for public bus transport is down over 11 per cent in real terms since 1979.

Bus fares have increased 77 per cent on average since 1979.

Services have been cut in many parts of the country. The

David Austin

Speech bubbles in cartoon:
WHEN DOES THE LAST BUS GO, INSPECTOR?
IN ABOUT A COUPLE OF MONTHS, MADAM.

National Bus Company's total mileage fell by nearly 10 per cent between 1979 and 1981 alone.

● Some communities have lost their services altogether. Many more have become virtual ghost-towns in the evenings and on Sundays.

● Rising fares, cuts in services, and the recession have driven away 15 per cent of passengers on the National Bus Company's network since 1979.

● Central government financial support for local authority transport—the Transport Supplementary Grant—has fallen by 10 per cent in real terms since 1979.

● The New Bus Grant—by which the government met half the cost of a new bus, and worth some £34 million in 1979 to the bus industry—is being rapidly phased out. It will go completely by 1984.

● The Transport Act has swept away many licensing provisions and encouraged private operators to start up services in competition with the public transport networks. Private operators are only interested in prime high-profit routes. Public operators, deprived of revenue from those routes, inevitably find it harder to continue with unprofitable services, which provide an essential lifeline to the communities they serve.

● New legislation—the 1982 Transport Act—allows the government to sell off the profitable parts of the NBC and so threaten the network further.

● A new Bill, aimed at restricting the scope for metropolitan counties to support public transport, has been introduced. London Transport's massive fare increases could hit other big cities.

Juggernauts

● Tory transport policy has led to an increase in the maximum permitted weight of lorries from 32.5 tonnes to 38 tonnes (for lorries with 5 axles), and to cuts in schemes for by-passes to keep heavy traffic away from towns and villages.

● Heavy lorries have not been paying for the damage they cause—in 1982-3 they will have underpaid by some £76 million.

Tory policies threaten the very existence of our rail network. Instead of diverting heavy traffic from road to rail, they actually intend to increase the burden on our already overcrowded roads.

Public asset-stripping

The Tories intend to break up public sector undertakings, selling off all or part of them.

● First to go in the transport sector was the National Freight Corporation (now Company). Half the shares in what was the British Transport Docks Board (now Associated British Ports) have been sold. The government has taken powers to sell shareholdings in British Airways. Powers to sell the profitable parts of the National Bus Company are also on the statute book.

● British Rail is being dismembered. Seaspeed Hovercraft has gone, so have most of British Transport Hotels. Disposals of Sealink is still on the agenda. Further privatisation—possibly of British Rail Engineering, possibly even of some actual rail operations—may also be in the pipeline.

These are costly deals for the taxpayer:

● **Associated British Ports**: the government wrote off £81 million worth of loans, then sold a valuable public asset for a mere £22 million. The price was so low that shares were oversubscribed more than 20 times.

● **British Airways**: cutbacks and redundancies have already been made to prepare it for 'privatisation'. The government could be faced with a bill of up to £1,000 million in writing off debts and other charges, for it to be saleable.

Personal social services

The number of people over 75—those who make some of the heaviest demands on services—is increasing by about 45,000 a year. Between 1978 and 1980 the number of children in care rose by nearly 5,000. And the economic recession has taken a heavy toll on family life in terms of poverty and insecurity. A 4 per cent increase in resources is needed each year just to stand still. Even the government recognises the need for a yearly increase of 2 per cent. Yet it has squeezed local authority budgets mercilessly and exhorted local authorities to reduce spending on the social services.

● Since 1980, four-fifths of Britain's local authority social service departments (SSDs) have been forced to reduce levels of provision. Forty-five per cent of English and Welsh SSDs have had to cut services per head by at least 7 per cent. And a tenth are now (1982-3) at least 15 per cent short of what they require to provide services at 1980 levels.

● Since 1980, the number of social workers (23,000 in England) has been frozen and the ratio of social workers to clients has deteriorated considerably.

● The House of Commons Select Committee on Social Services in 1982 heard evidence that '*most services for the elderly have not been maintained at a constant level of service over the past four years. Meals and home help services have scarcely grown in volume terms and almost certainly insufficiently to meet the growing demands... care places have fallen in proportion to the population over 75 since*

1979-80.' As the committee commented: '*There is widespread recognition that the care of the frail elderly represents the major challenge in personal social services over the decades ahead; that we should already be falling behind cannot but be disturbing and bodes ill for services to the elderly in future years.*'

● Residential care—old people's homes, children's homes, hostels for the mentally ill and handicapped—has also been cut. In 1982-3, 78 per cent of English and Welsh SSDs did not have the resources to meet increased demand. Fifty-four per cent of them experienced real cuts in income for residential care. In 14 per cent of the departments these cuts were 5 per cent or more.

● Nine hundred day-care places for the young physically handicapped were cut in England between 1979 and 1981 —a reduction of 9 per cent.

● The provision of special telephone attachments for disabled people was cut by 12.5 per cent between 1979 and 1981. Only 1,400 disabled people are now provided with these attachments by social service departments. As the Association of Directors of Social Services has pointed out: '*In the first round of cuts in 1979-80, the budget for giving aids and adaptations for the physically handicapped was a natural target for almost every local authority that had to make cuts. Thus causing great problems now (1982) several years later.*' Overall spending in that year on aids for disabled people fell by nearly 8 per cent over the previous year.

● The number of free TV licences for disabled people has been savagely cut—by more than half between 1979 and 1981. SSDs removed help with TV licences from over 24,000 disabled people in that period.

Charges

The Tories' cuts in the Rate Support Grant have encouraged some local authorities to introduce, or massively increase, charges for certain services.

● In 1981-2, England's SSDs raised £306 million from the old, the disabled and the deprived in charges for social services—31 per cent more than 1979-80.

● Between April 1981 and April 1982, one-third of SSDs increased day-nursery charges by more than the rate of inflation. Seven per cent of departments increased charges by more than 30 per cent. This was on top of increases made the previous year when 29 per cent of departments had increased charges by more than 30 per cent.

● Charges for meals on wheels went up in at least 43 per cent of SSDs in England and Wales in 1981-2. In 7 per cent of these departments charges rose by over 30 per cent. This followed increases of 30 per cent or more in two-thirds of the departments the previous year.

● In 36 per cent of English and Welsh SSDs home help charges were increased by more than 30 per cent in 1980-1. Further increases were made by 21 per cent of departments the following year.

Crisis in housing

Housing in Britain improved steadily over the last fifty years. Slums were cleared. Local authorities built up a stock of homes allocated to meet needs. New houses were built faster than old ones decayed. Homes without amenities were improved. That was until the Tories took over. Since 1979:

● Housebuilding has fallen to its lowest level since the 1920s—except for the war and immediately after—while nearly 400,000 building workers are on the dole.

● Housing is not being properly maintained—problems are being stored up for the future.

● Council rents have more than doubled—while subsidies to home-owners have increased.

● House mortgage payments have risen by a quarter.

● Councils have sold off their best homes—only the better-off can be sure of a decent home in the future.

Our future has been mortgaged for short-term political ends. **The result is a dire housing crisis.** In England and Wales alone there are:

● Over 1,207,000 unfit dwellings and 994,000 dwellings lacking one or more basic sanitary amenities. An estimated five million people live in them.

The housing stock is decaying faster than it is being repaired or replaced:

● Nearly four million dwellings in England require repairs of over £2,500, including a million over £7,000.

● One million industrialised and semi-industrialised dwellings are increasingly subject to building failure.

● Two-and-a-half million dwellings in the UK are estimated to be seriously affected by damp.

The adverse effect of these conditions on people is not quantifiable. Even figures of

● 800,000 households living in overcrowded conditions
● 800,000 households living in shared accommodation
● unknown thousands of homeless people

cannot convey the human misery involved.

The crisis affects everybody: home-owners, council tenants on run-down pre-war and system-built estates, private tenants, and newly forming households.

The Tories' housing strategy is to create a 'property-owning democracy', regardless of the social consequences. It is being executed through:

● cuts in public housing investment
● compulsory sales of council houses
● rising rents
● 'ghettoisation' of council housing
● revival of the private rented sector

The Tories have cut Labour's 1979-80 plans for investment in housing by over half in real terms.

● New public housebuilding has slumped—from 107,400 homes started in Great Britain in 1978, to 52,300 in 1982. It hit rock-bottom in 1981—at 36,900.

● Total housebuilding has fallen by a third. An average of 181,000 homes have been started in the last four years compared with 295,000 in the previous four years.

● Council house renovations have dropped—from 76,000 in 1979, to 62,800 in 1982.

● Council mortgage loan money is down—from £260 million

in England in 1979-80, to £55 million in 1982-3 in cash terms.

● Money allocations to councils assume capital receipts from sales (£511 million in 1979-80; £1,815 million in 1982-3, in England alone). This forces councils to sell houses and land on the open market, and so reduce their ability to provide new homes in future.

Tight government controls on housing programmes have resulted in councils not being able to spend as much as £0.5 billion of the money allocated to housing.

There have been savage cuts in subsidies to council tenants. The Tories have:

Slashed the government's contribution—from £1,423 million in 1980-81, to £370 million for 1983-4 (England).

Forced rents up to compensate for the loss of subsidy.

Increased mortgage tax relief—from £1,450 million in 1979-80, to £2,150 million in 1982-3 (estimated).

Increased the maximum mortgage on which interest is paid free of tax—from £25,000 to £30,000 in the 1983 budget. The cost: £60 million a year.

Council rents have been pushed up from an average £6.40 per week in 1979, to £14.45, in 1983-4 (estimate). Many Tory councils have pushed them up even higher. Rents in Kensing-ton and Chelsea will be £28.47 from April 1983.

● Rents now subsidise the rates in dozens of local authority areas, because the Tories have abolished the 'no-profit' rule for council housing.

Over three million tenants cannot afford to pay the high rents, and receive housing benefit help.

Tenants on housing benefit have had their budgetary freedom taken away, as their benefit is credited on their rent account.

Rents can now cost more than mortgage repayments on council homes.

Compulsory sales of council houses
The dramatic rise in rents is encouraging tenants to buy their homes. Discounts of up to 50 per cent and mortgage

concessions add further incentive. Nearly 500,000 sales have been made since the Tories came to power. Sales:

Cream off the best of the housing stock: forty-five houses are sold for every flat.

Create friction on estates between tenants who buy and those who do not.

Add to estate management problems.

Undermine the potential of councils to provide a good standard of housing for those who need or want to rent.

Increase the level of public subsidy: average tax relief per mortgagee is £327 a year, compared with a subsidy of £206 per council tenant.

It takes eleven sales to release enough cash for one new home to be built.

Housing Associations are also being compelled to sell:

non-charitable associations, following the Housing Act 1980;

charitable associations under proposals in the Housing and Building Control Bill.

Their revenue subsidies are being phased out, and rent rises speeded up. The real value of money allocated for new and improved homes to rent has been eroded, while that for homes for sale increased:

Approvals to start schemes for homes for rent have *gone down* from 39,414 in 1978-9, to 22,706 in 1981-2 in Great Britain. In England they went down from 31,791 to 19,450 and there were only 12,136 approvals in the first nine months of 1982-3.

Approvals to start schemes for homes for sale have *gone up*—from 405 in 1978, to 6,307 in 1981-2 in Great Britain. In England they went up from 365 to 6,138.

The Tories are intent on reviving the private rented sector. They have:

Loosened controls on security of tenure by creating insecure shorthold fixed-term tenancies, and by refusing to outlaw bogus 'holiday lets' and other Rent Act dodges.

Subsidised new housing built by private builders,

building societies and insurance companies for letting on assured tenancies at market rents.

● Pushed up rents for unfurnished accommodation—from an average £433 per year in 1978, to £740 in the second half of 1982, and from £679 to £1,116 for tenants in furnished accommodation.

The government is under pressure from backbenchers and the property world to abolish rent controls altogether, or at least to relax them still further. Yet:

● 370,000 private rented dwellings (17.7 per cent) in England are unfit for human occupancy.

● 282,000 (13.5 per cent) lack one or more basic amenities.

● 875,000 (42 per cent) need repairs in excess of £2,500.

Home-ownership has increased under the Tories—from 54.1 per cent of households at the end of 1978, to 56.4 per cent at the end of 1981. But:

● Disrepair is increasing fastest amongst owner-occupiers —21.3 per cent in England alone.

● 483,000 unfit properties, nearly half of the total, are owner-occupied.

● The average monthly mortgage rate under the Tories has been 13.25 per cent, compared with 10.74 per cent under Labour.

● The mortgage rate hit its highest level at 15 per cent between November 1979 and December 1980, and between October 1981 and March 1982.

● Compulsory sales of council housing have reduced the number of new buyers on the open market.

● Owners who need to become tenants have fewer chances because councils are prevented from buying their property.

● Owners do not really own their homes until their mortgages are paid off. Mortgage repayment arrears have more than doubled between 1979 and 1982. Homes repossessed by building societies because of arrears went up from an estimated 2,530 in 1979 to 5,320 in 1982.

In England alone, the number of households officially recognised as being **homeless** rose by 27 per cent from 53,110 in 1978, to 67,704 in 1981. The number deemed 'intentionally' homeless rose from 2,520 in 1981, to 3,020 in 1982.

Construction

The combined effect of the Tories' cuts in public housing investment, the general recession and compulsory council house sales has been disastrous for the **construction industry**.

● The number of private houses started in Great Britain slumped—from 157,300 in 1978, to 98,000 in 1980, and revived to only 140,600 in 1982.

● The number of construction workers on the dole has increased—from 160,000 in May 1979, to 389,000 in May 1982.

Pressure from the construction and housebuilding companies and the shock revelations of growing disrepair among home-owners forced the Tories to alter their strategy in 1982. The results have been:

● A slowing down in the housing investment cuts, to an estimated 2 per cent between 1982-3 and 1983-4.

● A redistribution of money underspent by some councils to those who thought they could spend more on building works by 31 March 1983.

● Easing controls on councils' housing programmes.

● Use of public money through councils and housing associations to buy homes from private housebuilders, and to resell them on a shared-ownership basis.

● Apparent easing of spending limits on home improvement grants while effectively limiting the amount that will be spent by insisting that only grants paid out by 31 March 1984 will be reimbursed.

Apart from deepening the housing crisis, the Tories are:

● Polarising society between the 'haves', who believe that home-ownership gives them a stake in society, and the 'have-nots', who are ghettoised into expensive and decaying council, housing association, and private rented housing. Council housing waiting lists grew 13 per cent between 1979 and 1981.

● Subjecting tenants who buy to the commercial restrictive practices that make home-ownership expensive and changing homes time-consuming.

● Creating a massive backlog of work to repair, modernise and replace decaying housing. It is estimated that £13,026 million should be spent in 1983-5 to clear the backlog.

Where there's (public) muck there's (private) brass

The Tories are eagerly promoting 'privatisation' of local services—paying private firms to clean the streets and collect rubbish. A myth-making propaganda campaign has been financed with Tory money. These are some of the myths:

'*Private contractors provide a better service.*' In the London Borough of Wandsworth refuse collection and street cleaning were contracted out to Pritchard Industrial Services. In the first week of operation there were 1,000 complaints. The company was fined £7,665 for falling below authorised cleaning standards. Then penalty clauses were suspended while the council trained Pritchard's in how to clean the streets. In Tory-controlled Sutton, only one road in seven was finished during a so-called 'blitz' clean—but the council had put no penalty clauses in the contract.

'*Councils will save money.*' Cleaning companies are offering attractive cheap deals as 'loss leaders' to tempt councils. For example, Southend quoted savings of £500,000 a year when cleaning was contracted out. But these figures hide the real costs because building and plant were sold to the contractors at a knock-down price. The contractors are out to make the biggest profit possible—so it is likely that the cost to the council will go up. In Southend, trade waste charges to companies and schools have doubled.

'*Workers will get a better deal.*' Experience shows that refuse workers, who already do a difficult and dirty job, face a big deterioriation in conditions. In Wandsworth some 'permanent' staff get only two weeks' holiday a year. Pritchard's provide no pensions and no sick pay during the first year of employment. Overtime is compulsory and it is obligatory to work five days out of any seven. Not all workers are taken on by the contractors—and it is usually the old, sick or trade union activists who lose their jobs.

In some cases of privatisation, there has been disturbing evidence of links between Tory councillors, consultants and the firms involved.

When the sums are done properly it becomes clear that local services are best provided by local councils. Even Tory councils—in Luton, Slough, Hillingdon, Chiltern, Fareham and Three Rivers—have rejected privatisation.

Rights reduced

We have now had four years of Tory freedom: freedom for businesses to close factories; freedom to move in search of the highest profit. Restrictions for the rest of us.

Rights at work and in the community have been eroded:

● Changes in industrial relations law have revived Gradgrind principles to tip the scales against workers and in favour of employers.

● The police are being given new powers to stop, search and hold suspects.

● Key government decisions are taken behind closed doors, with no moves towards freedom of information.

● The new Nationality Act—based on racist and sexist principles—strips citizenship rights from many people.

● Black people in Britain face official harassment and persistent discrimination.

Rights at work

The Employment Acts of 1980 and 1982 mean that:

● **Your right to strike has been restricted.** Trade unions are protected from civil actions only in 'trade disputes'. The definition of a trade dispute has been narrowed to cover only matters 'wholly or mainly' related to a dispute between an employer and his or her own employees. That rules out essential forms of trade union activity, such as sympathy action and solidarity boycotts.

● **You can be sacked more easily.** You now have to work for an employer for twelve months—it used to be six—before you are protected by the unfair dismissal laws. In a firm with fewer than twenty workers, you have to wait for two years. The Tories have also made it difficult to prove unfair dismissal—particularly in small firms—and abolished the minimum compensation award of two weeks' pay. Where ten to ninety-nine workers are being made redundant, your employer need now give only thirty days' instead of sixty days' notice.

● **You can be sacked for going on strike more easily.** Protection against unfair dismissal has been amended to allow employers to discriminate against strikers.

● **Your rights to a decent wage have been eroded.** You can no longer oblige your employer to pay the 'going rate' for your trade, because Schedule 11 of Labour's Employment Protection Act has been abolished. Workers on public sector contracts will no longer be protected by the 'Fair Wage Resolution' from September 1983. The Tories have also threatened to abolish the wages councils.

● **Your ability to defend your pay and skills by agreeing with your employers that they should employ union members only has been weakened.** Where such 'closed shop' agreements have been reached, ballots of all workers must take place every five years from next year and an 80 per cent majority is needed for the arrangement to continue. Workers who ride on the backs of other workers by refusing to join a union and lose their jobs as a result can now claim compensation of up to £20,000—for which the union may be liable. Those dismissed between 1974 and 1980 can claim compensation from the taxpayer.

● **Your rights to bring effective pressure on your employer in an industrial dispute have been weakened.** Only the employees of a company can take part in pickets of that company's premises. And you cannot now picket customers and suppliers of your employer to persuade other workers to help you. Breaking these rules can mean a hefty fine or even imprisonment.

● **Your trade union (and its officials) can be sued.** Up to £250,000 damages can now be awarded to anyone who can claim to have suffered a financial loss from many trade union activities. This is a return to Victorian legislation repealed as long ago as 1906. (Individual trade unionists have always been subject to the full weight of criminal law and to civil law for matters outside trade disputes.)

● **Women can no longer claim the same job back after having had a baby.** You still have a right to return to work on equivalent terms and conditions—but only if you fulfil new written notification requirements. If your employer has fewer than six workers, even this right is removed.

The Tory Green Paper on 'trade union democracy' foreshadows another series of attacks:

● Compulsory ballots before strike action, which could make it very difficult to respond immediately to changes.

● A switch to a 'contracting in' system for trade union contributions to political activity. This could cut funds for Labour, while big business's contributions to the Tories remain untouched.

● No-strike clauses for workers in 'essential' public services —an idea floated in the 1981 Green Paper on trade union immunities.

● Interference in union affairs to force ballots in union elections.

The Tories like to pretend that their approach to industrial relations will bring industrial peace. In fact the number of working days lost through strikes has *increased* by 30 per cent, from 796,000 a month under Labour to 1,035,000 under the Tories.

Rights in the community

In the last four years the state's powers have been vastly extended at the expense of individual rights.

Police powers

Instead of attempting to build a relationship between the police and the community which might help prevent crime and give reassurance to victims, the Tory government has predictably opted for more police, more police hardware and greater police powers.

Since the urban riots of 1981, plastic bullets and CS gas have been authorised for police forces and a Bill proposed for stronger police powers. The Public Order Act has been used more frequently to ban marches.

The Tories' Police and Criminal Evidence Bill:

● Greatly increases police powers to stop and search

people in the street, to arrest suspects, and to set up road blocks.

● Extends the time a suspect can be kept in police custody after arrest, but before charge, to ninety-six hours, forty-eight of which could be without access to a lawyer.

● Allows the police to fingerprint children over the age of ten without their consent or the agreement of a magistrate.

● Enables the police to get a warrant to search the home or workplace of a person *not suspected of an offence* in order to find evidence of a 'serious' offence. The police will be able to search the premises and confidential records of advisers such as doctors, psychiatrists, priests, social workers, etc.

The Bill even fails to implement the safeguards recommended by the Royal Commission on Criminal Procedure for Suspects. Most important, the Bill:

● Does not replace police responsibility for prosecutions by an independent public prosecutor.

● Does not provide for increasing accountability of the police to the public or their elected representatives.

The forerunner to this Bill, the Scottish Criminal Justice Act 1980, also contains a hotch-potch of measures which seriously threaten the liberty of the individual, places at risk the principle of policing by consent and yet offers no evidence that it will reduce crime.

The Criminal Attempts Act 1981 rightly scrapped Section 4 of the Vagrancy Act 1824 (the old 'sus' law) but created a new offence—interference with vehicles—which has perpetuated many of the objectionable features of 'sus'.

The objection to 'sus' was that it made it criminal merely to *intend* committing a crime. The new offence makes it criminal to 'interfere' with a motor vehicle in a public place 'with the intention of' gaining entry to it, or access to anything in it, or to discover 'whether it is possible to gain such entry or access'. In other words, anyone seen leaning on a car or looking inside by the police can be picked up as on 'sus'.

Security services

Surveillance—the collection of personal information, the use of informers, telephone tapping, the interception of letters, and so on—is effectively uncontrolled by law. The great extension of police capability in the area over the last few years has taken place with no legal restraint and no effective public supervision.

Labour's attempts to make our security services more accountable have been consistently blocked by the Tory government. It has voted down:

- Robin Cook's Security Services Bill
- Frank Hooley's Freedom of Information Bill
- Bob Cryer's Interception of Communications Bill

Yet a series of spy and security services scandals, involving among others Anthony Blunt, Roger Hollis (ex-director of MI5) and Geoffrey Prime (a Russian agent at the government's communication headquarters) has pointed up the need for closer public scrutiny and greater efficiency. Such scandals also expose age-old double standards—Geoffrey Prime, an ordinary employee formerly at the Communications Headquarters, received thirty-five years for spying, while Anthony Blunt, for years a 'member of the establishment', was granted immunity by MI5.

Prevention of Terrorism Act

The 1976 Prevention of Terrorism Act is another example of excessive executive power—in particular its system of exclusion orders. Introduced in the wake of the Birmingham pub bombings in 1974, the Act allows citizens *believed* to be connected with terrorism to be excluded from the UK. It gives the police the power to arrest suspects and to detain them without charge for forty-eight hours, on their own authority, and for a further five days with the authorisation of the Secretary of State. The suspect is not charged with a criminal offence and has no right to a trial or to an appeal against the decision, though representations may be made to a government-appointed adviser.

Only a tiny proportion (5 per cent) of those detained under the PTA have been charged, yet the Tories still support its continuation. A recent review under Lord Jellicoe even suggested that some of its powers should be extended to cover international terrorists of any group, cause or nationality. In March 1983, William Whitelaw made it clear that the government backed Lord Jellicoe's major recommendations and that he would be introducing new legislation to that effect.

Prisons

Britain's prisons are overflowing. In 1975 Roy Jenkins, then Home Secretary, warned that the system would become intolerable should the prison population reach 42,000. Since 1979, the average daily prison population has exceeded that figure. It is now over 44,000. In July 1981 it reached an all-time record of 45,500 in accommodation meant to house fewer than 39,000. About a third of all prisoners—especially in local prisons—live two or three to a cell designed for one, for up to twenty-three hours a day. Often there is no integral sanitation, necessitating 'slopping out', and no proper access to educational, recreational or work facilities.

> 'We have become decreasingly able to meet virtually any of the objectives expected of us other than the simple "incapacitation" of the offender for the period of his sentence. Certainly there is no evidence that prison has either any systematic deterrent or rehabilitative effect.'
> Report on the Work of the Prison Department, 1981

Imprisonment has always been an expensive and inefficient response to crime: it costs more than £9,000 a year to keep a person locked up. On release prisoners are more embittered and less able to cope than before. Recidivism is high: half of all male prisoners commit an offence within two years of being released. The Home Secretary's one imaginative proposal—to release some prisoners after serving one-third of their custodial sentence and to require them for the next third to be under constant supervision out of prison—has been abandoned. Instead, under the Criminal Justice Act 1982 he will introduce a system of partially suspended sentence. The modified proposal may actually increase the prison population if judges give partially suspended sentences in place of a straightforward suspended sentence.

In addition, Whitelaw has failed to remove from the prison system those people everyone agrees should not be there—petty offenders, fine defaulters, alcoholics and the mentally disordered. Nor has the government acted to reduce the scandal of those in prison on remand—in many cases innocent men and women have to wait six months for the opportunity to demonstrate their innocence. But most important, since it could have the biggest effect on the prison population, no legislation has been introduced to reduce maximum sentences. The Dutch cut their prison population by half in the 1950s by reducing prison terms and have experienced no greater increase in the crime rate.

Instead of such action, the government intends to concentrate on providing a net increase in new and refurbished prison places. Expensive and time-consuming, such proposals will have no immediate impact on overcrowding and poor conditions.

Young offenders

The Tory approach to young offenders is confused and misguided. The Criminal Justice Act 1982, which deals mainly with the sentencing of young offenders, has several welcome aspects, such as giving the courts greater powers to pass non-custodial sentences. But it represents a lost opportunity for radical change. Following the introduction of a tougher regime—'a short, sharp shock'—at four detention centres in 1980 and 1981, the Act allows courts to impose short sentences of between three weeks and four months on young male offenders. These centres place emphasis on 'discipline, tidiness, self-respect and respect for those in authority', combined with 'drill, parades and inspection' and provide less education and fewer useful skills. There is no evidence that their tough regimes are more productive than borstal or detention centres where reconviction rates run high—78 per cent and 72 per cent respectively within two years for boys under 17. It is right for the courts to pass shorter sentences wherever possible but it may lead the courts to give a larger number of young boys the taste of imprisonment who would not otherwise have been given a custodial sentence.

The right to know and be not known

The Tory government says it favours 'freedom', but has taken no action to introduce a Freedom of Information Bill which would provide for open government and place the onus on public authorities to justify withholding information. On the contrary. In its first year it introduced a Bill which Stuart Patrick described in the *Daily Mail* as 'honestly and unashamedly devoted to the belief that government is a secret process and that the press and public should be told only what Whitehall considers good for them.' The Bill was so widely criticised it was withdrawn.

British citizens remain completely unprotected by law against the collection and use of personal information. The Tories have introduced a Data Protection Bill in the House of Lords, but only in order to conform to a Council of Europe Convention. It covers only computer-held records and not unusual data files, and even then there are many exemptions. The Bill has been criticised by bodies as diverse as the British Medical Association, the National Council for Civil Liberties, the Law Society and the National Consumer Council.

Nationality and immigration

According to the last Tory manifesto, 'the rights of all British citizens are equal before the law whatever their race, colour or creed', and 'their opportunities ought to be equal too'. In practice, Tory policies have been designed to appease the racists.

Nationality. We need a positive statement of British nationality which defines the connection between the individual and the state and establishes rights and obligations on both sides. Instead, the Tories produced the British Nationality Act 1981, whose main preoccupation is to remove possible sources of future immigration—at all costs.

Under the Act, citizenship of the UK and colonies is scrapped and replaced by:

● *British citizenship*, which gives freedom to enter and remain in this country to all, mostly white, who were 'patrial' under the 1971 Immigration Act, that is people whose parents or grandparents were born, adopted, naturalised or registered in the UK, and citizens of the UK and colonies who are settled and have been here for five years.

● *Citizenship of the British dependent territories* for non-patrials, almost entirely black. This gives no right of entry to Britain, but can be expected to give a right of entry to a Dependency under its immigration laws.

● *British overseas citizenship*, also for non-patrials, which gives no right of entry to the UK and no automatic right of entry anywhere.

Khormek '83

Plans to allow women as well as men to bestow citizenship on their children, and to let citizens retain dual nationality, are welcome. But there are other disturbing, discriminatory aspects of the legislation. The Act makes it more difficult to acquire British citizenship by:

Birth. Children born in the UK will be British citizens only if at least one of their parents is a British citizen or is lawfully settled here. In practice the Act will result in elaborate checks on the immigration status of parents before passports are issued, thereby creating more opportunities for racial harassment.

Registration. Commonwealth citizens settled here before 1973 and wives of British citizens will lose their automatic right to British citizenship five years after the law comes into effect. The Tories have retained the Home Secretary's discretionary powers, instituted no right of appeal against refusal and appear to have no intention of reducing the delays or the high cost of naturalisation—which has been increased from £90 to £200 (by 120 per cent) since they came to power.

Immigration. In their 1979 manifesto, the Tories stated that one of their five main tasks was 'to support family life'—but not, it seems, the family life of Britain's black population: Under the *Immigration Rules* of 1980 and the changes made to them in 1983—a compromise between a ruling of the European Court of Human Rights and the demands of the Tory racists—women who are British citizens, not just settled here, have the right to bring their husband or fiancé to live here with them. This applies only if immigration officials are satisfied that the marriage partners have met, that the primary purpose of the marriage is not to gain entry and that they intend to live together permanently as man and wife.

The new rule is sexist—the right of men settled here to marry foreign women and to bring them to this country has never been questioned; racist—it is mainly directed at men from the Asian sub-continent; and indefensible because for the sake of reducing the number of black immigrants by between two and three thousand it will cause intense suffering through separating husbands and wives.

Before they can be admitted to this country, children between eighteen and twenty-one years old, and elderly parents, have to show that they have no other relatives to turn to, that they are dependent and that they have a standard of living substantially below the average in their own country.

The rules also increase the insecurity of migrant workers and overseas students living here.

Internal controls

Black people's status in Britain has been undermined not only by immigration controls at the port of entry. There has been an ominous increase in internal control under the Tories.

The government has continued to remove large numbers of alleged illegal entrants—590 in 1979, 910 in 1980 and 640 in 1981—and has extended the definition of illegal entry to people who were wholly ignorant of the deception which made them illegal entrants, and who have lived and worked here for many years.

The Home Office has gone to extreme lengths to uncover illegal entrants. A number of police and immigration service raids for illegal immigrants have taken place: lawfully settled citizens have been wrongly arrested and detained until they had proved the legality of their presence. One of the most notorious, at Bestways, in May 1980, resulted in the unlawful detention of twenty-eight Asian workers.

Black people must prove the legality of their presence here not just in relation to immigration control. Increasingly, other agencies are requiring them to do so. The introduction of charges for NHS treatment for 'overseas visitors' in October 1982 has meant that the eligibility of foreign-looking patients for free treatment is frequently questioned. In social security offices passport checks are also routine for 'persons who appear to have come from abroad', and an arrangement exists for suspected illegal entrants to be reported to the Home Office.

Such checks will inevitably extend the opportunities for racial harassment and increase the feelings of insecurity among black communities.

Racial inequality

The Tories' official line is that there must be stringent immigration control as well as equal rights and equal opportunities for all British citizens irrespective of race or religion. In practice, the Tories have eagerly adopted tougher policies on immigration while doing virtually nothing to eliminate racial inequality and protect black people from violence. Perhaps this is not surprising from a party that opposed Labour's 1976 Race Relations Act and failed to take up Labour's 1979 Local Government grants (Ethnic Group Bill) when they came to power.

After four years of Tory rule—and inaction—the ethnic minorities still face:

● *Discrimination in employment* A CRE report published in 1980, based on research completed in Nottingham in 1979, showed that discrimination against black applicants for white-collar jobs occurred in nearly half of the one hundred firms tested.

● *Discrimination in housing* Research in Nottingham in 1981 revealed that 40 per cent of council house applicants of West Indian origin were allocated flats compared to 21 per cent of white people; 43 per cent of applicants of West Indian origin were allocated houses compared to 60 per cent of whites. Black house-buyers also have to search longer and harder for a mortgage than whites do, according to Leeds Community Relations Council.

● *Educational disadvantage* Many reports reveal that ethnic minority children, especially those of West Indian origin, are not deriving the benefit that they should from our education system. For example, the Rampton Committee Report 'West Indian Children in Schools' revealed that in English Language, only 9 per cent of West Indian pupils gained an O level pass compared with 20 per cent of Asians and 19 per cent of other leavers.

Black people are also physically under threat. According to a Home Office estimate in 1981 there were then a minimum of 7,000 racially motivated attacks a year. It is believed that these attacks are running at a rate of between 10,000 and 20,000 a year. Yet no action has been taken by the government or the police authorities to curb this violence. Even Scarman's recommendation that racially prejudiced behaviour should be made a police disciplinary offence has been rejected.

Northern Ireland

Tory government has been a disaster for the people of Northern Ireland:

● Talks between the British and Irish governments on closer co-operation between Britain and Ireland have effectively ended.

● No progress has been made towards the establishment of an agreed devolved government.

● A toothless Assembly has been set up, boycotted by representatives of the minority community. This is lowering respect for constitutional politics.

● The economy, with unemployment over 20 per cent and living standards drastically cut, is in tatters.

● Since May 1979, unemployment has almost doubled —from 10.7 per cent to 20.6 per cent. In some areas, like Strabane, it approaches 40 per cent.

● Draconian security powers, such as the Prevention of Terrorism Act and Emergency Provisions Act, have restricted civil liberties and proved largely ineffective against terrorism.

● Since 1979, seven people, including four children under the age of sixteen, have been killed with the plastic bullets sanctioned by the government.

Life in the 1980s

Thatcher's Inner city

The Tories have aggravated the already critical problems of the inner city—high unemployment, poor housing, and heavy concentrations of people with special problems. They have:

● Eroded the statutory town and country planning system, weakened public consultation and introduced charges for planning applications.

● Cut off £1,000 million of central government money for inner-city areas; and shifted the bias in the rate support grant towards the Tory shires. Many inner-city authorities are being penalised as 'overspenders'.

● Reduced council housebuilding to its lowest level since 1924 and cut housing investment by half since 1979.

● Cleared out and destroyed jobs. Set up enterprise zones to allow businesses to operate with fewer controls, and urban development corporations in London and Merseyside Docklands to override the local authorities.

● Repealed the Community Land Act, leaving local authorities without effective land purchase powers at the same time as taking powers to privatise land publicly held by local authorities, new towns and statutory bodies.

Rural rides

Margaret Thatcher swept the countryside in 1979. She repaid her rural voters with job losses, decimated bus and train services, unbuilt houses, closed schools, and cut services.

The Tories slashed public expenditure in the rural areas by 3 per cent in real terms between 1981-2 and 1982-3.

'I would resist demands for any massive injection of government or local authority assistance [to rural areas] —even if it were available, which it is not.'

Michael Heseltine, then Secretary of State for the Environment, 1980

● Rural unemployment is often way above the national average:

Northumberland	14.8 per cent
Cornwall	17.5 per cent
Western Isles	25.5 per cent

● In 1979, twenty-five village schools were closed; in 1981, seventy-nine.

● The Tories have cut new housebuilding in rural districts by nearly half—16,400 completions in 1981 compared with over 27,000 on average in the mid-1970s. Over 80 per cent of houses completed were in the private sector—compared with a national average of only 54 per cent.

● The Tories' Transport Bill, which 'deregulated bus services', has led to a massive cutback in the rural bus network—150,000 operating miles lost in Lincolnshire and an 11 per cent loss in North Yorkshire in 1981-2 alone.

● Rail links are also under threat because of the Tories' refusal to allow British Rail to invest in these services.

● Higher fares and reduced rural transport have also made it harder to find work.

● The vital services provided by rural sub post offices are under threat as a result of the Rayner Review on the payment of benefits. Telephone kiosks are threatened by plans to privatise British Telecom.

Poison finger

The quality of the environment has no place in the profit and loss accounts of a Tory Britain:

● **Pollution Control**: We agree that the Control of Pollution Act is

'likely to have greater and more lasting effect on the quality of life than most other measures, we shall do all we can to assist its passage onto the statute books.'

Margaret Thatcher, 17 June 1974

After four years of Tory rule, major parts of the act remain unimplemented.

● **Clean Air**: The Tories have abolished the Clean Air Council and cut grants for anti-pollution equipment by almost half.

Lead in petrol: The Tories have been pushed into a partial reduction of lead in petrol (0.4 grammes per litre) by the EEC. Labour proposed an outright ban.

Noise: The Tories abolished the Noise Advisory Council in the 'quango cull' of 1980.

Waste: The Tories have abolished the Waste Management Advisory Council, wound up the 'Swop-shop' of the Waste Materials Exchange, and have not yet required local authorities to produce a plan for waste.

Nuclear energy: The Tories have embarked upon the largest capital spending programme ever in peacetime—the £15 billion Pressurised Water Nuclear Reactor Programme, despite continued doubts about nuclear safety, falling energy demand, and overcapacity. Cabinet minutes reveal that such a programme 'would have the advantage of removing electricity production from disruption by coal miners'.

Energy conservation: The Tories have cut real spending on local authority conservation and on conservation advertising. Research and development spending on conservation remains minimal.

This sporting life

Sport and leisure are fast becoming luxuries. The Tories have:

● Ordered local authorities to lower swimming-pool temperatures by 2°C.

Directed local authorities to sell off their sports and playing fields.

Contributed to the 10 per cent drop in people watching sport since 1979 by increasing VAT on spectator tickets by 90 per cent.

Reduced the use of community facilities, such as schools, by cutting local government funds for staff overtime.

Undermined on-course betting by increasing betting duty—which has also meant an 800 per cent increase in illegal betting.

Threatened to introduce charges for entry into museums.

Keeping politics out of sport?

● The Tories tried to stop Sebastian Coe, Steve Ovett and the rest of the British team from going to Moscow for the 1980 Olympics as part of the new cold war. But they have made it easier for South African sportsmen and women to tour in the UK.

The arts

Before the last general election, Margaret Thatcher promised there would be 'no candle-end economics' in funding the arts. Yet:

'There is little economic security for the arts today. The recent reductions in real terms in the government's grant aid to the Arts Council, have forced us to make unpleasant cuts to clients in 1981-3.'

The Arts Council Annual Report, 1981-2

The Arts Council was £10 million short of what the Council estimated to be 'the realistic minimum needs of the Arts'.

The government is increasing its political control of the arts:

● Sir William Rees-Mogg, former editor of *The Times*, and Margaret Thatcher's old ally, has been rewarded with the chair of the Arts Council as well as the vice-chair of the BBC.

● People like the vice-chair, Professor Richard Hoggart, who were not part of the 'establishment', have been kicked out.

● Luke Ritner, another Tory, has been made secretary-general despite strong protests from the Council's staff and the art world in general. His only qualification is that he is administrator of the Association of Business Sponsorship for the Arts. In true Tory philistine tradition, public support for the arts is giving way to commercial patronage.

Cosh and baton

Tory policy on law and order has been an abysmal failure. They have certainly spent more—£4,284 million in 1982, as against £2,579 million in 1979—but this has had little effect.

● Serious crime increased by 30 per cent in the first three years as compared with a rise of 22 per cent in the previous five years. There are now 8,200 serious crimes recorded every day, or 342 crimes every hour—a crime every ten seconds—and according to the Home Office's own recent crime survey, many offences go unreported.

● Detection has plummeted. The number of solved crimes fell from 42 per cent in the last full year of Labour government to an appalling 38 per cent in 1981.

> *'If boys and girls do not obtain jobs when they leave school, they feel that society has no need of them. If they feel that, they do not see any reason why they should take part in that society and comply with its rules. That is what is happening and, wherever we sit in this House, that is what we have to recognise.'*
>
> William Whitelaw, then Shadow Home Secretary, 27 February 1978

If that was true in 1978, when there were 1½ million unemployed, it is—in spite of Tory denials—even truer today. This is not because the unemployed are criminals but because unemployment leads to poorer social conditions, even broken families, and it is these factors which lead some of those affected to become involved in crime.

Britain in the world

Defence – apocalypse soon?

The Tories have taken crucial decisions which will turn Britain into the densest nuclear arsenal in the world. Far from making Britain safer, their defence policy has brought war closer. Far from reassuring the country, six out of ten people now believe nuclear war to be possible where four out of ten did only twenty years ago.

● Britain spends more of its income on war and preparing for war than any major country apart from the USA and the USSR: 5.3 per cent compared with 4.1 per cent in France, 3.4 per cent in Germany and 2.6 per cent in Italy.

● This year, the Tories plan to spend £16,000 million on the military—£20 a week for every family of four.

● The Tories are spending 33 per cent more on defence than on education—under Labour more was spent on education than on defence.

● In five years, the Tories will have upped real military spending by 23.3 per cent. At the same time, they have *cut* spending on housing by 55 per cent, on education by 6 per cent, on overseas aid by 20 per cent, and have presided over the biggest drop in output for sixty years.

Nukes

The Tories have helped push the nuclear arms race into a new and dangerous phase. They have decided to upgrade the British independent nuclear deterrent by phasing out the ageing submarine-launched Polaris missiles and replacing them with Trident missiles, also launched from submarines. And they are allowing the USA to install a new breed of weapon—the cruise missile—on British soil.

These decisions bring us nearer to the brink. Both Trident and cruise are designed to fight nuclear wars, not just deter them. They make it inevitable that worldwide military spending will accelerate.

If the Tories get back:

● The nuclear element in the defence budget could increase by half over the next five years, from 8-10 per cent now to 13-17 per cent in 1988.

● At best, £20 billion will have been committed over the next forty years to a single weapon system—Trident—£9-11 billion over the next twelve years.

● Britain's nuclear arsenal could more than double —possibly treble—over the next twelve years. The current total of 1,700 warheads and bombs could rise to more than 2,800.

● By 1995, Britain will have stocks of nuclear warheads equivalent to ten tons of TNT for every man, woman and child in the country and a concentration of nuclear destructive power per square mile five times the current US density.

● By 1986, the USA will own and control half of the nuclear weapons on British soil and ships—up from the current 45 per cent.

● Between 1980 and 1990, Britain will have more than doubled the number of aircraft with a nuclear strike capacity to 412. Sixty new Harriers will have been built at a cost of £8 million each—£480 million (at 1982 prices) in total.

● Britain will be a major launching-pad for US cruise missiles, the weapons system at the heart of the new cold war.

The Tory Trident Programme

The Tories intend to build four large nuclear-powered submarines as platforms for the Trident missile. The submarines—each twice the size of the current Polaris submarine, or three times the size of an average destroyer—will be constructed in the late 1980s. They can carry a total of sixty-four missiles armed with up to 896 warheads.

Trident warheads are super accurate: they are weapons not for simple deterrence but for fighting nuclear wars. Many governments, including the Soviet, believe they might be used for a pre-emptive attack (first strike). The *fear alone* will fuel a new arms race.

Trident could increase the number of separate Soviet targets which Britain could destroy from sixty-four to 896—a fourteen-fold increase on the existing Polaris.

Cruising to suicide

Cheap cruise missiles with their many, highly accurate nuclear warheads, are the greatest threat to verifiable disarmament agreements.

The Tories agreed to the USA stationing cruise missiles in Britain late in 1979; ninety-six to be placed in Greenham Common, Berkshire, by December 1983, and a further sixty-four at Molesworth, Cambridgeshire, by 1986.

Each missile carries a 200 kiloton warhead (16 times the size of a Hiroshima-type bomb) and is extremely accurate—to within 100 yards of a target 1,500 miles away.

The cruise missiles are US-owned and controlled. They are mobile and their deployment will increase the US nuclear arsenal in Britain by 26 per cent (from 124,000 kilotons to 156,000 kilotons). They will make Britain more vulnerable to nuclear attack because they are *counterforce* nuclear warfighting weapons designed for fighting a limited nuclear war, and because they arouse justifiable fears of a pre-emptive attack.

UKA

Britain is the USA's largest unsinkable nuclear missile and aircraft carrier. Apart from the cruise missile programme there are already in position:

• Some 156 F1-11 long-range bombers stationed at Upper Heyford, Oxfordshire, and Lakenheath, Suffolk. Each is capable of delivering between four and six nuclear bombs (deployment of the new EF1-11 jamming aircraft will enable F1-11 to be effective to the end of the century).

- Between eight and ten Poseidon submarines at Holy Loch, Scotland, each with sixteen missiles and each of those with ten 40-kiloton nuclear warheads—altogether with the destructive power of some 64 million tons of TNT.
- More than 100 US-controlled nuclear depth charges for British Nimrod aircraft patrolling the Atlantic.
- Several hundred nuclear shells for US nuclear artillery based in West Germany, stored at Burtonwood in Lancashire.

There's money for...

£	would buy	or provide
£2,500 million	1 Trident nuclear submarine with missiles	an extra £1 a week on child benefit for 5 years
£180 million	1 Type 42 destroyer	8 new district hospitals
£35 million	1 Hunt Class minesweeper	5 new telephone exchanges
£8 million	1 Harrier jump jet	16 new primary schools
£3 million	1 Lynx helicopter	120 new council homes
£7,000	1 Milan anti-tank missile	1 kidney machine
£100,000 a year	3 generals	10 teachers or 15 nurses or 20 home helps or 25 college places or 125 nursery school places

Military myths: 1
The Tories want multilateral disarmament

The Thatcher government has:

- Refused to allow its Polaris nuclear missiles to be included in either of the Geneva negotiations on intermediate

nuclear weapons or strategic nuclear weapons.
- Opposed, with the USA, proposals from India, Sweden and Mexico for a United Nations freeze on the deployment, testing and production of all nuclear weapons.
- Refused to take up the proposals from the Palme Commission and the Swedish government for a battlefield nuclear-weapons Free Zone in Europe.
- Unilaterally escalated the arms race by its commitment to Trident.
- Undermined the Nuclear Non-Proliferation Treaty by holding fast to the so-called independent nuclear deterrent.
- Condoned the USA's new chemical weapons rearmament programme and its decision to produce the neutron bomb.
- Refused to pledge that it will not use nuclear weapons first in any conflict.

Military myths: 2

The British Medical Association believes that:

- Direct casualties of a nuclear war would be 2½ times the official estimate, or over forty milion dead. Survivors would be vulnerable to starvation, disease, lack of medicines and safe water.
- The entire NHS could not cope with the casualties from one single-megaton bomb, let alone the 200 megaton attack envisaged by the Home Office.

Yet the Tories:

- Have stepped up spending on 'civil home defence preparedness'—from £27 million, to £45 million in 1983-4.
- Are pledged to new regulations which will, for the first time,
    * force *all* councils, county, district and borough, to provide war-time headquarters and equipment, and take part in exercises like 'Hard Rock' (planned for 1982 but postponed indefinitely because of public opposition);
    * force councils to recruit, train and exercise every civil defence volunteer—training on the rates for strikebreakers?;
    * conscript, in effect, workers into nuclear war planning without consulting the unions.

Military myths: 3

Each new leap in the arms race has been sold to the public with the single threat—the Russians are ahead; if we don't catch up they might attack us. A recent poll found that 55 per cent believe this. Yet the truth is that, in almost every type of weapon, the west is ahead.

- *Strategic nuclear warheads*. The USA has a total of 9,268 and the USSR an estimated 7,300.
- *Submarine-launched nuclear warheads*. The USA has 4,768 to the USSR's estimated 1,800.
- *Tactical nuclear warheads in Europe*. The USA has 7,000 with another 10,000 that could be quickly flown in. The USSR has a maximum of 6,000 in European USSR.
- *Long- and medium-range theatre nuclear warheads in Europe*. NATO has 1,999. The Warsaw Pact countries have 2,297.
- *Conventional ground forces in Europe*. NATO has total forces of 2.1 million. The Warsaw Pact countries have 1.7 million.
- *Total forces* on the NATO side amount to 5.3 million. The Warsaw Pact countries have 4.8 million in their armed forces.

These simple statistics ignore the fact that in almost every system the NATO weapons are technologically superior.

The Falklands Tragedy

'*A new government was elected in Britain just over a year ago. That government, of which I am proud to be a member, is making the most fundamental changes to the economic and industrial fabric of the country probably since the second world war—and those changes bear a remarkable similarity to the changes being made by the government here.*'

Cecil Parkinson MP, then Minister of Trade,
speaking to business people in the
Argentine capital of Buenos Aires, August 1980

'*Why did Argentina's rulers suddenly decide... to resort to... aggression? Part of the answer lies in the very brutality and unpopularity of the Argentine regime itself. The regime is*

notorious for its systematic contempt of all human rights.'
Francis Pym MP, Foreign Secretary,
speaking in the House of Commons, 7 April 1982

On 2 April 1982, Argentina invaded the Falklands—a British dependency—in pursuit of a longstanding claim to sovereignty. A naval task force of 112 ships was sent from Britain to add to economic and political pressure on the Argentines to withdraw. Britain went to war for the first time in twenty-six years. After bitter fighting, the islands were recaptured. Two hundred and fifty British servicemen died. Almost 800 were wounded. Well over a thousand Argentines were killed or wounded. The total cost of the war and defence of the Falklands up to 1986 will be nearly £3,000 million—over £3 million for each family on the island.

The tragedy could have been avoided:

● *The government signalled that Britain was not serious about defending the islands* when it announced, in December 1981, that *HMS Endurance* would be withdrawn from South Atlantic duty. The Tories also denied many of the islanders full British citizenship under the 1981 Nationality Act.

● *The government failed to read clear signs from Argentina* that imminent military action was a real possibility. Press reports from inside the country, reports from the British ambassador in Uruguay and an abrupt change in the Argentine negotiating position all pointed to the dangers.

● *When the danger was recognised no action was taken.* Margaret Thatcher told her advisers to make contingency plans at the beginning of March. None was made. The cabinet's Defence Committee did not even discuss the issue.

Tory policy now is to fortify the islands and ignore the need for a long-term settlement—'Fortress Falklands'. That means keeping some 4,000 troops on the islands and spending £424 million on garrison costs in 1983-4. With Argentine claims undiminished, no peace can be secure. While most people believe that Britain must restore normal links between the Falklands and the Latin American mainland and that the United Nations must be involved in finding a permanent international settlement of the problem, the Tories are sticking their heads firmly in the sand. With them in charge, the danger of further hostilities in the

South Atlantic is very great. To Tory incompetence, however, has been added Tory hypocrisy, for the Tories are now allowing:

● *The refinancing of Argentina*. The government is allowing some thirty British banks to provide $260 million to bail out the debt-ridden military junta. No guarantees have been given that the money will not be used to buy weapons.

● *The rearming of Argentina*. Although Argentina refuses to declare formally that hostilities have ended, the government is permitting British companies to supply components for Exocet-carrying Argentine warships.

Exporting scorched earth

There are now 800 million people in the world condemned to a life of squalor, malnutrition and misery; a life of *absolute* poverty. Some 40,000 children die *each day* from lack of food, safe water and medical care. In over thirty countries, the average life expectancy is less than fifty years (two-thirds the OECD average).

That poverty has been greatly intensified by the world economic crisis. Many poor countries, with few natural resources and exploding food and energy bills, have piled up enormous debts. Even some of the better-off countries, such as Mexico and Brazil, are now so deeply in debt that the stability of the world's financial system is threatened. Economic expansion has been squeezed out in all but a few isolated pockets of the developing world.

Yet the Tories have:

● **Substantially reduced economic aid**—by 16 per cent in real terms, to 0.44 per cent of national income. That falls far short of the UN and Brandt aid target of 0.7 per cent and contrasts starkly with the Netherlands' 1.0 per cent, Sweden's 0.8, or France's 0.7.

● **Reduced the quality of British aid**. Under the Aid-Trade Provision, the Tories now give over £50 million per year as inducements to foreign governments to buy British. £5 million went on an airport in the Turks and Caicos islands to complement a holiday village which was never built.

● **Shifted aid to exceptionally oppressive regimes**. One of the largest recipients is the dictatorship of Turkey (£20 million in 1981); authoritarian Paraguay and the Philippines are also now beginning to enjoy Tory generosity.

'Our aid is exceptionally well spent.'

Geoffrey Howe, Chancellor of the Exchequer,
22 October 1982

● **Combined with the Reagan administration**. Together the two governments thwarted major pro-Third World initiatives such as 'global negotiations' at the UN.

● **Refused to endorse the United Nations Convention on the Law of the Sea**. Designed to preserve the wealth of the open seas as 'the common heritage of mankind', the Law of the Sea was a major advance in international co-operation. It was opposed by the Reagan administration and US-based multinational mining companies.

● **Rejected the Brandt Commission's 'North-South—A Programme for Survival'**. This put forward an emergency programme of measures covering aid, trade, finance, food supply and energy. Former Tory Prime Minister, Edward Heath, is a member of the Brandt Commission.

● **Resisted calls for world reflation**. The Tories refused Third-World demands for improvements in the policies and practices of the International Monetary Fund and the World Bank, on which it depends for much of its finance.

● **Abolished the Development Education Programme**. Under the last Labour government, this scheme stimulated public interest in development issues.

Blarney in Brussels

The Tories' willingness to accept Community policies as given has added to Britain's industrial and economic decline. Rather than seek reforms, as hinted at in their manifesto, they have consistently supported the most reactionary elements in the EEC, leaving us in a worse position.

● Despite Thatcher's early bluster, Britain remains the second-largest net contributor to the EEC budget even though we are one of the poorest members of the Community in income per head. In 1982, the Community cost us more than £620 million net. The government did manage a temporary reduction in our contributions—at the cost of increased food prices, an unacceptable fishing regime and a whole list of other concessions.

● Between 1979 and 1982, our deficit on trade in manufactured goods with the rest of the Community grew—from over £3,000 million to about £5,000 million, more than 60 per cent. Our trade surplus with the rest of the world increased 22 per cent—from over £4,000 million to over £5,000 million.

In employment terms, our deficit in manufacturing with the EEC cost 500,000 jobs.

● Instead of the radical changes they promised to effect in the EEC's agricultural regime, and a commitment to freeze prices, the Tories have accepted ever-increasing price hikes: 1.5 per cent in 1979, 2.4 per cent in 1980, 9.5 per cent in 1981, 10.5 per cent in 1982. By agreeing these rises, the Tories have dashed any hopes of reforming the Community.

In all, it has been estimated—by the Tory MP Richard Body—that the Common Agricultural Policy cost British consumers £3,000 million in 1982—£5 per week for every family.

● The Tories sold out over the Common Fishing Policy. They failed to deliver a twelve-mile exclusive zone and a twelve-to-fifty-mile 'zone of dominant reference'. They accepted a deal which gave UK fishing fleets only 36 per cent of the catch in UK waters despite the fact that over 60 per cent of EEC fish stocks are in UK waters, and failed to ensure proper policing of the quotas.

General support in Turkey

On 12 September 1980, a military coup brought to power a ruthlessly repressive regime. By January 1983, there were 27,818 political prisoners, a further 9,817 were awaiting trial, some 3,000 of whom faced the death penalty. These included fifty-two leading trade unionists and twenty-six peace campaigners. Two hundred people have been 'shot resisting arrest'.

The Tories have:

● Refused to back a move by a number of European countries to refer Turkish human rights violations to the European Commission of Human Rights.

- Opposed the removal of Turkey's vote on the Council of Europe.
- Welcomed the authoritarian constitution thrust upon the Turkish people in November 1982. Despite clear intimidation of voters in the referendum ratifying the constitution, the Tories labelled the voting 'both fair and secret'.
- Provided Turkey with totally disproportionate amounts of economic aid at a time when other countries were withholding aid. In 1981, Turkey received 4 per cent of our bilateral aid (some £20 million)—more than Zimbabwe. Yet Turkey's per capita income was more than twice that of Zimbabwe.

Reagan's poodles: the Tories in Central America

- **Guatemala** Denounced by international and local human rights organisations, and in dispute with British-garrisoned Belize. *Tory Britain refuses to condemn the well-forged links with its main supporter and arms supplier, the United States.*
- **El Salvador** Main instrument of US-backed repression in the area, *condoned by Tory Britain*, whose two observers of the bogus elections (March 1982) were the sole official representatives to break a European boycott.

'*The election complicated the political problems of the country, made life worse for the people in it, and has caused the deaths of people who, without the election, would now be alive.*'

Lord Chitnis, Liberal,
reporting to the Parliamentary Human Rights Group

- **Nicaragua** Main focus of US-backed aggression in the area, *abandoned by Tory Britain*.

The South African connection

Just prior to the last general election the *Financial Times* assessed the views of the Foreign Secretary, Francis Pym:

'*Mr Pym does not believe there is anything to be gained

from publicly putting pressure on South Africa to end or even reduce apartheid... He thinks that Southern Africa is strategically important and that public pressure should be taken off.'

This view was endorsed by Margaret Thatcher when, as Prime Minister, she expressed her desire to 'make progress towards ending the isolation of South Africa in world affairs'. The view has been matched by action:

- The ban on backdoor North Sea oil exports to South Africa has been lifted.
- The UN mandatory arms embargo was flouted by the export of a mobile radar system, manufactured by Plessey.
- The public naming of companies paying starvation wages in Africa was ended.
- The British veto was used to protect South Africa from censure in the UN Security Council.
- An IMF loan to South Africa of £622 million was approved.

What the Tories have done to you

What the Tories have done to women

'I don't think that mothers have the same right to work as fathers. If the good Lord had intended us to have equal rights to go out to work, he wouldn't have created man and woman.'

Patrick Jenkin,
Secretary of State for Social Services,
'Man Alive', October 1979

'The battle for women's rights has been largely won.'
Margaret Thatcher speaking to women in London,
26 July 1982

Though the Tory 'model' family with Dad as breadwinner and Mum at home looking after two children accounts for only 5 per cent of all households, government policies are based on the view that married women— except for a privileged few like Margaret Thatcher—have no right to paid employment. So the married women who make up one-quarter of the labour force and especially those—about half—who are caring for at least one dependent child have done particularly badly in Thatcher's Britain. They have had to face:

● **A large increase in unemployment**. Female unemployment is well over two million. Even government statistics, which ignore non-claimants, most of whom are married women, admit to 900,000 women, half a million up on the May 1979 figure.

● **Greater difficulty in claiming unemployment benefit**. Mothers must show they can make arrangements for their children while out at work before they are eligible.

● **A worsening in pay compared to men**. The progress made as a result of Labour's Equal Pay Act has been reversed. Women's earnings as a percentage of men's rose from 63.1

per cent in 1970 to 75.7 per cent in 1977, and then fell back to 73.9 per cent in 1982.

● **Low pay**. Women, who form 40 per cent of the workforce, now make up three-quarters of the low paid. They have been disproportionately affected by changes in the Employment Protection Act, the abolition of the Fair Wages Resolution, and the weakening of the wages councils.

● **Poorer terms of employment**. The 1980 Employment Act attacked women's right to paid maternity leave and to protection from dismissal because of pregnancy. The government refuses to act on the suggestions made by the Equal Opportunities Commission and TUC to strengthen the Sex Discrimination and Equal Pay Acts.

● **Reduced educational and training opportunities**. If women are to break into traditionally male-dominated occupations they must get positive educational help. But the brunt of the education cuts has been borne by women. Increasing class sizes, the shortage of mathematics and science teachers, inadequate book provision and the reduction in in-service training have limited the ability of schools to develop girls' capacities to the full and to overcome the sexist bias of the education system. In post-school education, the approaches which help women most are the first targets for economies: mature student places, the Open University, day release, TOPS and other vocational courses, essential to those who have missed out on education or need retraining, have all been cut. And there are practically no apprenticeships for women—only hairdressing takes on a steady number—while new technology is threatening many clerical and secretarial jobs.

The proposed introduction of student loans would further deter women: the strong social pressures that prompt them to finish education early, marry and have children, would be compounded by the strain to repay.

● **Cuts in social security benefits**. Women account for two-thirds of pensioners, most of the seven million recipients of child benefit and 27 per cent of the unemployed on the official count. They have suffered disproportionately from the Tories' decision not to protect benefits from inflation.

● **Exile to the home**. Disappearing community services are forcing women with family ties to give up their jobs and look after the old, the young and the sick. Although single parents suffer most, all families are affected. After increasing by an unprecedented 17 per cent between 1977 and 1980, the real income available to families dropped by 6 per cent since the end of 1980.

What the Tories have done to black people

'People are really rather afraid that this country might be rather swamped by people with a different culture. People are going to react and be rather hostile to those coming in.'
Margaret Thatcher, giving the green light to the racists, 30 January 1978

Four years of the Tories have meant:

● **Worse unemployment.** In 1981, when 9 per cent of white people were out of work, joblessness among non-white groups was *twice* as high, at 17 per cent. A recent survey by the Commission for Racial Equality found that 53 per cent of teenagers of West Indian origin compared with 37 per cent of white teenagers are now out of work in inner-city areas.

● **Continuing discrimination and disadvantage in jobs, housing and schooling.** Black applicants for white-collar jobs are less likely to be successful than white applicants with similar qualifications. In many local authorities, black families are likely to be allocated worse housing. Building societies are more reluctant to lend to black people. Children from ethnic minorities do not achieve their full potential in schools. The Tories have done nothing to strengthen the Race Relations Act or to eliminate racial inequality.

● **Harassment with official approval.** New NHS charges for overseas visitors mean that 'foreign-looking people' are asked to prove they are eligible for free treatment. Police raids in search of illegal immigrants have led to the detention of lawfully settled citizens. The government rejected the recommendation in Lord Scarman's Report on the Brixton riots in 1981 that racially prejudiced behaviour should be made a specific offence under the police disciplinary code.

91

● **Increased danger of racist attacks**. The Home Office estimate that at least 7,000 racist attacks occur each year, a figure they believe to be 'on the low side'. There has been, they conclude, 'a fairly steady rise in the number of attacks reported since about 1977 and a marked rise since 1980.'

● **Families divided.** The Tories' 1980 Immigration Rules and the 1981 Nationality Act have separated husbands from wives, children from parents and elderly relatives from families. In one recent case Rustam Khan faced deportation to Pakistan and separation from his wife and two children. The children were born here and Mrs Khan is permanently settled, as are her parents, brothers and sisters.

● **Reduced citizenship rights**. Commonwealth citizens who came to Britain before 1973 no longer automatically acquire British citizenship. They must apply through an expensive procedure. Wives of British citizens and children born in the UK are also deprived of automatic citizenship. People who previously had rights as 'citizens of the UK and colonies' but who were not classified as 'patrials' have had most of these rights taken away. Some 1½ million people, now given 'third-class' British overseas citizenship, are left effectively stateless—they have no legal right to live anywhere.

What the Tories have done to young people

After four years of Tory government, there is:

● **Little chance of a job**. Fewer than one in two school leavers will find work this year. Forty per cent of the unemployed are under the age of twenty-five—1.2 million people.

● **Exploitation on 'training schemes'**. Under Labour, the Youth Opportunities Programme offered a bridge between school and work. Now it is just a gang plank to long-term unemployment. YOPsters work for £25 a week receive little training and have just a one-in-three chance of getting a job at the end.

● **Less chance of training**. Apprenticeships have fallen to

60 per cent of the 1979-80 level. The Tories have abolished sixteen of the twenty-three statutory industrial training boards. The Youth Training Scheme which replaces YOP in September 1983 is a step forward, but there is doubt that sufficient places with adequate training will be made available for sixteen-year-olds, and many seventeen-year-olds will not be eligible.

● **Less chance of higher education**. Around one in six places at universities and polytechnics are being cut. Colleges are asking for higher qualifications as competition hots up.

● **A lower standard of living**. The Tories took away the right to claim supplementary benefit for two months in the summer after leaving school. They have kept allowances on YOP down to £25, a 16 per cent cut in their real value over four years. And their Young Workers' Scheme is aimed at reducing wages—employers are being bribed with a subsidy to pay young people less than £40 a week. Student grants have been cut by 10 per cent in real terms.

● **Fewer youth clubs**. Spending on the youth service has been cut by 4 per cent in real terms. The number of youth leaders and wardens fell from 4,730 to 4,480 in the Tories' first two years.

What the Tories have done to elderly people

'The government's overall priority is to reduce and contain inflation... As the economy improves elderly people will share in that improvement. In the meantime we have to hold back public spending and concentrate on the revival of the economy.' Government White Paper, 'Growing Older', March 1981

The Tories have certainly held back from doing any good to Britain's pensioners. 9.5 million people have lost out.

Pensions

The Tories broke the link between pension increases and the rise in average earnings. As a result, married pensioners have lost £2.25 a week and single pensioners £1.45 since 1979.

Services

Many elderly people, and especially the very elderly, depend upon local authority services to retain their independence and self-respect. Government cuts in the Rate Support Grant to local authorities have prevented the number of home helps, meals on wheels, day-centre places and other services from keeping up with rising demand.

The government has offered just £6 million over three years to improve health services for the elderly mentally ill—£133,000 per year for each regional health authority. A drop in the ocean, given the scale of need.

Fuel poverty

Since May 1979 electricity prices have risen by 84 per cent and gas prices by 115 per cent. Many elderly people are at risk from the cold. On average 48,000 more people over sixty die in the winter months than in the summer.

Many elderly people are now forced to choose between eating and heating. But the Tories scrapped Labour's Electricity Discount Scheme which gave help to those on rent and rate rebates as well as to those on supplementary benefit. Now only pensioners receiving supplementary benefit can receive help with fuel bills.

Public transport

Fewer pensioners own cars than the rest of the population. For them, public transport is vital for getting about, but the Tories are busy undermining the ability of local authorities to provide good, cheap public transport.

● Their 1980 Transport Act enabled private operators to cream off the best routes, jeopardising the future of less profitable, but no less essential, routes.

● Their 1982 Transport Bill will force many authorities to abandon 'cheap fares' policies, and the Tories do not intend to adopt Labour's plan for a national scheme of concessionary travel for the elderly and the disabled.

What the Tories have done to disabled people

'*The disabled cannot expect to be exempted from the sacrifices necessary [for economic recovery].*'

Minister for Social Security and the Disabled,
at the Royal National Institute for the Blind.

'*The International Year of Disabled People comes at a time when there are no resources available for significant improvements in benefits or services.*'

Patrick Jenkin,
Secretary of State for Social Services

Living standards

Apart from the 183,000 recipients of mobility allowance—about 10 per cent of the significantly handicapped population—disabled people have seen benefits fall in value and, in some cases, have experienced actual cuts.

● Attendance allowance, industrial disablement benefit, invalidity benefit, non-contributory invalidity pension, invalid care allowance, which increased under Labour in line with the rise in prices or earnings, whichever was the greater, are now protected only against inflation. Disabled people are thus denied any share in the future prosperity of the country. During 1981, this meant a loss of £31.20 for a severely handicapped person in receipt of the higher rate of attendance allowance.

● Invalidity pensions—paid to about 600,000 people who are too disabled to work—have also been cut by 5 per cent. A married invalidity pensioner is now £4.25 a week worse-off than under Labour. A married invalidity pensioner with two children is £6.15 a week worse-off.

● Industrial injury benefit, for those unable to work due to an industrial accident or disease, is abolished as from April 1983.

● Before the revised supplementary benefit scheme introduced in November 1980, about two-fifths of disabled claimants used to receive a single payment for exceptional needs in any one year. These grants are no longer available except in very limited circumstances.

Unemployment

Disabled people face an unemployment rate 50 per cent above the average and are three times as likely to be unemployed for more than a year. Yet the Manpower Services Commission plans to cut the number of disablement resettlement officers by 120 up to 1985.

Community services

Community services are as important as benefits in determining the living standards of many disabled people. Yet:

● Between 1979-80 and 1980-1, expenditure on aids and adaptations telephones and holidays for disabled people fell from £4.5 million to £4.2 million.

● Some local authorities are disregarding their statutory obligations under the Chronically Sick and Disabled Persons Act to provide services for those in need, but the Secretary of State has been reluctant to act against them.

● The number of new council homes started for disabled people in 1980 was down by 32 per cent—compared to an average cut in council house starts of 23 per cent.

● In July 1981, a government Green Paper on 'Care in the Community' proposed various ways in which 15,000 mentally handicapped and 5,000 mentally ill people could be moved from hospitals to the community. Early in 1983, the government issued a circular explaining why most of the initiatives could not be pursued and emphasising that 'progress now depends on making better use of what is already available'.

Education

No new money was made available for the provision in the 1981 Education Act to integrate children in special schools into ordinary schools. This affects 185,000 children.

What the Tories have done to families with children

Over the past four years, children and their parents have suffered a major attack from the self-styled 'Party of the Family'.

● Since 1979 the number of children living on supplementary benefit—the 'official' poverty line—has increased by 90 per cent to 1.75 million. Many millions more are living on the margins of poverty, including at least 306,000 children in families claiming family income supplement.

● The number of working families caught in the poverty trap has doubled to 130,000 since 1978.

● The number of children living in families where the head of the household is unemployed doubled in the two years to December 1982. There are now around 1.5 million such children. Yet the government has cut child support for the unemployed by more than a fifth, or £1.70 a week, since 1979.

● Child support for all families has been cut. Child benefit is now worth 25p a week less than when Labour left office. The increase scheduled for November 1983 will do no more than restore the level Labour was planning for November 1979.

● In 1973, Margaret Thatcher promised nursery places for 90 per cent of four-year-olds and 50 per cent of three-year-olds by 1982. Tory plans today are to *reduce* the proportion of three- and four-year-olds in nursery education—from 39 per cent in 1979-80, to 35 per cent by 1985.

● Local authorities are no longer required to provide a meal of a certain nutritional value for all their school children. Meanwhile charges for school meals have risen from a standard charge of 25p in 1979 to an average of 50p in 1983, and the government has scrapped the national scheme of free school dinners for families on low incomes. Only children from families on supplementary benefit or family income supplement now have the right to free school meals.

● The government's Family Policy Group is now planning an even bigger assault on families. They would 'encourage mothers to stay at home'. If all mothers did so, the number of families in poverty would increase four-fold. They would also introduce education vouchers and so increase public subsidies to private schools and create greater inequalities in the level of education provision.

And for her next trick...

If the Tories *do* form the next government, this is what they have set themselves to achieve.

More on the dole

All the economic forecasters say unemployment will go on rising if Tory policies continue. The optimistic ones say it will peak in 1984 or 1985. If the present policies continue, output

'is projected to grow by 1.5 per cent a year on average over the next five years. This is barely sufficient to maintain employment. Unemployment continues to edge up, reaching 3.75 million (on the old basis) by the end of the period.'

National Institute of Economic and Social Research, November 1982

Supermarket schooling

● The Tories threaten to introduce supermarket schooling with vouchers which could be used to pay for private education.

'A voucher system is one possibility.'

Sir Geoffrey Howe, 3 July 1982

'I am intellectually attracted to the idea of education vouchers.'

Sir Keith Joseph, 17 December 1982

● Student grants are likely to be replaced by loans, making it even more difficult for students without family backing to go to college.

Panorama, 28 February 1983

'Student loans are another possibility.'

Sir Geoffrey Howe, 3 July 1982

● Technical education could be developed into a separate

stream in secondary schools, breaking with the comprehensive principle.

Richard Lindley: *'So the idea would be to have two streams of education in schools—separate but equal?'*

Sir Keith Joseph: *'Separate but equal, intertwined... intertwined.'*

Panorama, 28 February 1983

Ill-health

● The Tories' 'Think Tank' proposed a system of private health insurance to replace the NHS.

'Private health insurance is already one of Britain's growth industries. We must encourage it to grow faster.'

Sir Geoffrey Howe, 3 July 1982

Fractured local government

● More services are likely to be hived off to private contractors:

'The more private individuals and businesses can be brought to perform some part of what is now performed by local government, the easier [the] problems will be to resolve.'

Sir Geoffrey Howe, 3 July 1982

● *'The abolition of the Greater London Council and the six other metropolitan county councils is now almost certain to have pride of place in the Conservative Party's general election manifesto.'*

The Times, 19 January 1982

Derailment of public transport

● The Serpell Report put forward options which could mean big fare increases, reduced maintenance and leave vast areas of the country without rail services—Wales beyond Cardiff, Scotland beyond Glasgow and Edinburgh, Somerset, Devon and Cornwall.

'We are looking at the whole range of options and the

Serpell Report has opened them up, I think, in a very valuable way.'

David Howell, Transport Minister,
24 January 1983

'Stay at home' women

● A Tory government should:

'Encourage mothers to stay at home.'
'[Determine] what more can be done to encourage families to reassume responsibility for the disabled, elderly, unemployed, 16-year-olds.'
'Review the effectiveness of the Equal Opportunities Commission.'

Cabinet Commission report leaked to *Guardian*,
17 February 1983

Trade union rights reduced

● The Tories are likely to bring in no-strike rules in some public services. The government could:

'Specifically prohibit strikes in the police force, the ambulance service, the fire brigade, nurse and/or medical staff, gas, water, electricity, nuclear power and sewage workers.'

Proposals from Tory Centre for Policy Studies,
Financial Times, 19 February 1983

● They plan an attack on union links with the Labour Party by changing the law governing payments of money for political purposes.

'This would best be done by substituting contracting in for contracting out.'

Green Paper, 'Democracy in the Trade Unions',
January 1983

● Wages councils, which now protect the lowest paid, are likely to be abolished.

'[There is a] widespread belief that the government intends to abolish wages councils when the International Labour Convention can be "denounced" in 1985.'

Financial Times, 4 March 1983

● Compulsory ballots before strikes are proposed.

Green Paper, 'Democracy in the Trade Unions'

More public asset-stripping

● *'State ownership and control should be displaced or supplemented, whenever sensibly possible, by the discipline and pressures of the market place.'*

Sir Geoffrey Howe, 3 July 1982

● Announced plans for privatisation include shares in British Telecom, British Airways, Sealink and British shipbuilders. Profitable parts of British Leyland, the National Bus Company, British Airways and British Gas oil interests and showrooms are likely to be sold outright. Other candidates for sale include Rolls Royce, the Forestry Commission and the vehicle testing centres.

'I have got a little list.'

Patrick Jenkin, Industry Minister,
5 October 1982

Nuclear PWR – no thanks

● Another Tory government will proceed with plans to build up to ten Pressurised Water Nuclear Reactors (PWRs) —the first at Sizewell. This is the American designed nuclear power plant which came close to disaster at Three-Mile Island.

Arms for arms' sake

● *'Last year we spent more on defence of western interests than any other country, apart from the United States. Next year we shall spend more again.'*

John Nott, then Defence Secretary,
5 October 1982

● Another Tory government will proceed to buy Trident missiles to renew Britain's 'independent' deterrent and continue to accept US cruise missiles—turning Britain into the most dense nuclear arsenal the world has ever seen.

Mrs Thatcher's Diary

May 1979

3 May: Tories win general election.
Jobs lost: ICI 1,200 over 3 years.

June 1979

First Tory Budget. Basic rate of VAT up from 8 to 15 per cent. Top rate of income tax down from 83 to 60 per cent and basic rate down from 33 to 30 per cent. Spending cuts of £2.8 billion.

Minimum Lending Rate up from 12 to 14 per cent.

Scotland and Wales Acts repealed, ending any plans for devolution.

Jobs lost: Inland Revenue 1,000.

July 1979

Cuts of over one-third in regional aid announced.

Price Commission abolished.

British Aerospace to be denationalised.

Energy Commission disbanded.

Education Act passed—allowing LEAs to continue selection.

Regional planning councils to be disbanded.

Jobs lost: British Steel 12,000.

August 1979

British Shipbuilders announce cuts of 10,000 jobs in merchant shipbuilding within 18 months.

Jobs lost: Perkins Diesel 7,000, Chrysler 2,000, Hoover 700-1,200.

September 1979

Post Office to be split into two separate corporations.

School meals charges increased from 25p to 30p.

Overseas student fees raised by 32 per cent.

Urban development corporations to be set up in London and Merseyside Docklands.

Fifty-seven 'quangos' axed.

Jobs lost: BL 25,000, Prestcold 1,000, GKN 1,000, ITT 900, Courtaulds 600.

October 1979

Exchange controls abolished.

Public stake in BP reduced from 51 to 46 per cent.

Jobs lost: Singer 3,000, International Computers 1,200.

November 1979

Public spending cuts of £3,500 million announced for 1980-1.

NEB Board resigns en bloc.

Protection of Official Information Bill abandoned after widespread criticism.

Interest rates up to a record 17 per cent.

Jobs lost: 40,000 civil service jobs to go over three years, Courtaulds 2,600, British Steel 2,000, ICI 2,000, Talbot 1,500, Massey Ferguson 1,500, Firestone 1,500, BSR 1,000.

December 1979

National Ports Council abolished.

National Enterprise Board sells public stake in ICL.

Expansion of nuclear power programme announced.

Five per cent devaluation of green pound.

New immigration rules approved.

Jobs lost: Harland and Wolff 1,200.

January 1980

Mortgage rate goes up to all-time record of 15 per cent.

Abandonment of 'Parker Morris' minimum standards for new council housing announced.

Jobs lost: British Steel 11,300, Lesney Products 7,500, Leyland Vehicles 750.

February 1980

School meal charges increased from 30p to 35p.

Manpower Services Commission budget cut by an additional £30 million a year from 1981.

Government-commissioned report published suggesting

break-up of ILEA (report rejected).

Funds for housing investment cut by a third.

Jobs lost: Laird Group 1,500, Massey Ferguson 1,000, Tootal 800.

March 1980

Tories' second budget. Sets out financial plan for spending cuts and monetary restraint over four years.

Public expenditure White Paper announces plans to halve public spending on housing between 1979-80 and 1983-4, and cut education expenditure by 9.5 per cent.

Enterprise Zone proposal announced.

Jobs lost: Laird 1,500.

April 1980

Prescription charges raised from 45p to 70p.

Education Act passed.

Jobs lost: Lucas Electrical 1,000, Courtaulds 750.

May 1980

Rate of inflation reaches 21.9 per cent—more than double the May 1979 level.

British Aerospace Act lays plans for privatisation.

Ian MacGregor appointed to chair of British Steel Corporation with 'transfer fee' of up to £1.8 million.

Jobs lost: Courtaulds 12,300, NCB 4,200, BCS 3,600, Talbot 1,300.

June 1980

Announcement of UK sites for 160 cruise missiles.

Gas Act.

Industry Act forces NEB asset sales.

Jobs lost: Lucas Electrical 3,000, Ilford 2,500, BSR 2,300, Ford 2,300, GKN 2,000, Alfred Herbert 1,343, Grundig 1,000, Burton 750, Levey Products 750, Courtaulds 660.

July 1980

Arms embargo of Chile lifted.

Sales of National Enterprise Board stake in Ferranti announced.

Weakening of the Post Office and Telecommunications monopolies announced.

Government announces decision to spend £5,000 million on 'Trident-1' as Polaris replacement.

Enterprise Zone sites announced.

Transport Act passed.

Announcement of setting up of holding company to 'privatise' British Rail subsidiaries.

Jobs lost: National Freight Corporation 1,000, Perkins 650, John Dickinson 630, BL Components 580.

August 1980

Unemployment goes over 2 million for first time in 45 years.

Employment Act restricts trade union rights.

Housing Act.

Government announces extra £45 million for civil defence for period 1981/2-1983/4.

Jobs lost: John Ayers 1,900, Bowater 1,600, Courtaulds 1,200, Reed Paper and Board 700, Massey-Ferguson 680, Hoover 440.

September 1980

Government announces £200 million cut in local authority grants for 1980-1, with extra penalties for 'high spending' councils.

British Rail and National Bus Company announce service cuts.

Jobs lost: CEGB 3,000, Girling 2,200, GKN 2,000, Metal Box 1,260, Royal Doulton 1,000, Courtaulds 700, BP Chemicals 400.

October 1980

Freeze on new local authority housing in England.

Jobs lost: British Steel 25,000, ICI 4,200, Evening News 1,750, Blue Circle 1,500, Perkins 1,200, Phillips 1,100, Goodyear 1,000, Firestone 600, GKN 644.

November 1980

Limit on public sector pay set at 6 per cent.

Community Land Act repealed, eroding public control of development land.

Contempt of Court Bill published.

Mini Budget: spending cuts and tax increases to save

£3,000 million.

Jobs lost: Talbot 3,500, ICL 2,500, Bowater 1,600, United Biscuits 1,500.

December 1980

Prescription charges up 30p to £1.

Council rents increase of £3.25 announced. Capital spending on council housing cut by 15 per cent.

Jobs lost: Leyland Vehicles 2,700.

January 1981

Green Paper on industrial relations published.

Jobs lost: Vauxhall 5,000, British Shipbuilders 3,200, Tate and Lyle 1,500, Fisons 1,000.

February 1981

Fifty per cent of British Aerospace shares, worth £150 million, sold.

Jobs lost: Talbot 4,800, Courtaulds 1,900, Firth Brown 1,250, Dupont 1,100, London Brick 1,100.

March 1981

Third Budget: special tax on windfall bank profits; income tax allowances not increased with inflation.

Privatisation of Cable and Wireless announced.

Jobs lost: Lucas Industries 4,500, BPC 2,750.

April 1981

National insurance contributions up 19 per cent to 7.75 per cent.

Jobs lost: Ford plans 29,000 job losses in 4 years, Lucas Electrical 2,100, Hadfields 1,900.

May 1981

Government grant to local authorities to be cut by £900 million.

Jobs lost: Burmah Oil 1,100.

June 1981

Defence White Paper. Navy to lose 30,000 jobs, army to lose 7,000. Chatham dockyard and base to close.

Riots break out on streets of Southall, Brixton, Man-

chester, Liverpool and many other cities.
Jobs lost: BR 16,000, ICL 5,200.

July 1981

University places to fall by 12,000 over three years.
Government holdings in British Sugar Corporation sold.
Riots in Toxteth, Liverpool.
British Telecommunications Act.
Employment and Training Act.
National Enterprise Board and National Research and Development Corporation merged to form British Technology Group.
Civil service strike called off after five months.
Jobs lost: Vauxhall 2,000, BP 1,670, British Enkalon 1,300.

August 1981

Jobs lost: Hoover 2,000, Imperial Tobacco 1,000.

September 1981

Jobs lost: British Airways 9,000, ICI 3,000.

October 1981

British Nationality Act—deprives many of citizenship rights.
Sale of Cable and Wireless shares.
Jobs lost: Rolls Royce plans 15,000 cut over five years, Hoover 1,800.

November 1981

Government plans to abolish 16 out of 23 Industrial Training Boards.
New public expenditure plans include rise in council house rents, and cut in real value of unemployment pay.
Jobs lost: Leyland Vehicles 4,100, ICL 1,500.

December 1981

Government launches Youth Training Scheme, to start September 1983.
GLC cheap fares ruled unlawful by Law Lords.
Government plans to cut local authority spending by 3.5 per cent; cut in real terms of £240 million from education budget.

Rise in national insurance surcharge announced.
Jobs lost: British Aluminium 900, Gallagher 800.

January 1982

Unemployment goes over 3 million. Young Workers'
Scheme started—employers subsidised for low-paid
young workers.
Jobs lost: Rolls Royce 600, Tootal 500.

February 1982

Amersham International sale—speculators make a killing.
Non-EEC overseas visitors to be charged for hospital
treatment.
Laker Airways goes bust.
National Freight Corporation sold to consortium of
managers.
Jobs lost: Laker Airways 1,700, BSR 1,400, Lucas
Aerospace 1,050.

March 1982

Fourth Budget maintains squeeze on the economy.
Capital gains tax softened by subtracting gains due to inflation.
Plans to buy Trident II missiles from USA for £7.5 million
announced.
Defence review White Paper proposes 10,000 redundancies in navy over five years.
Jobs lost: Imperial Tobacco 1,700, British Aerospace
1,200.

April 1982

Argentina invades Falklands.
Task force sent.
Prescription charges rise from £1 to £1.30.
Reorganisation of British Airways paves way for sell-off.

May 1982

Senior civil servants and army officers get 14.3 per cent
pay rise. Judges get 18.69 per cent.
Jobs lost: De Lorean 1,300, British Aerospace 950.

June 1982

Falklands recaptured. Ceasefire on 14 June.

Oil and Gas (Enterprise) Act passed to prepare way for privatisation of parts of BNOC and British Gas.

'Assisted area' status removed for several regions.

Proposals to privatise government research and development establishment.

July 1982

Multimillion pound defence purchase programme announced.

Abolition of National Water Council announced.

Plans to privatise British Telecom announced.

Eleven new Enterprise Zones created.

HP controls abolished.

Jobs lost: British Airways 7,000, British Shipbuilders 1,500, GEC 800.

August 1982

Jobs lost: British Steel Corporation 1,122.

September 1982

Leak of Think Tank plans to privatise NHS.

October 1982

Pay target of 3.5 per cent set for public sector.

Transport Act.

Jobs lost: RHM 1,300.

November 1982

Mini budget: employers' national insurance surcharge cut 1 per cent; Chancellor proposes to 'claw back' 2 per cent of value of pensions and benefits by failing to cover inflation in 1983.

Jobs lost: British Steel Corporation 3,000, GEC 600, Babcock 480, GKN 440, STC 400, Metal Box 215.

December 1982

Government proposes £31 million development plan for Falklands.

New defence orders for £1 billion to replace equipment lost in Falklands.

Jobs lost: Michelin 4,000, BSC 2,200, BSR 1,100, GEC 600, GKN 550.

January 1983

Serpell Report floats ideas for big cutbacks in British Rail.

Announcement of rise in prescriptions from April from £1.30 to £1.40.

Green Paper on 'union democracy' published.

Jobs lost: British Shipbuilders 2,300, Ford 1,300, BSC 630, Lucas Girling 550.

February 1983

Public expenditure White Paper: 3 per cent increase in defence spending.

Sale of shares in Associated British Ports.

Jobs lost: BR proposes 3,800, British Alcan 1,200, Distillers 530, Aurora Holdings 200.

March 1983

Budget: small income tax concessions; hidden cut in pensions; nothing to reduce unemployment.

Jobs lost: Littlewoods 1,900, 1,000 dockers from various ports, Woolworth 500.

April 1983

National insurance contributions up 9 per cent.

Sources_____

1. Introducing Thatcher's Tories _____

Sources for each point in the Tory record are given in the relevant section below.

2. The New Depression _____

Basic sources are:

- The *Department of Employment Gazette* for unemployment, employment and price figures.

- *Economic Trends*, from the Central Statistical Office (CSO) for investment, output and living standards.

- *Financial Statistics*, (CSO) for the money supply, public borrowing, interest rates, exchange rates, company liquidations and bankruptcies.

- The *Monthly Digest of Statistics* (CSO) together with the annual *UK Balance of Payments* and CSO and Department of Trade press releases for figures on imports, exports, industrial production and overseas investment.

- The *Bank of England Quarterly Bulletin* for estimates of changes in effective competitiveness and import penetration.

- Comparisons with the 1920s and 1930s are based on figures in *Economic Growth in Twentieth Century Britain* by Aldroft and Fearon.

- International comparisons are derived from the *OECD Economic Outlook*, *OECD Main Economic Indicators* and *IMF Financial Statistics.*

- Evidence on ethnic minority unemployment (page 9) is found in the *Department of Employment Gazette* of June 1982 and reports from the Commission for Racial Equality. Low pay and unemployment are linked by a study by the DHSS published 26 October 1982.

- Estimates of the costs of unemployment (page 10) are based on MSC figures published on 8 November 1981. The links between ill health and joblessness were exposed by

Harvey Brenner in the US and Donald Fagin in the UK. See *Labour Weekly* 18 July 1980.

- The failure of the Young Workers Scheme (page 10) was exposed by a report from the Institute of Manpower Studies in March 1983.
- A thorough critique of monetarism (page 11) can be found in *The Scourge of Monetarism* by Lord Kaldor.
- Yesterday's People (page 13) is drawn from press reports and research by Peter Chippendale.
- International comparisons of investment (page 16) are calculated from a written answer in Hansard 26 July 1982. Evidence on research is from the OECD report on the UK February 1983.
- Forecasts referred to on page 17 are by the Treasury, London Business School and National Institute for Economic and Social Research.
- The estimated cost of privatisation on page 21 is given in a written answer in Hansard 28 October 1982.

3. Rich and Poor
Basic sources are:

- *Economic Trends* (CSO) for information on living standards.
- *Department of Employment Gazette* for prices and earnings and average earnings.
- The *New Earnings Survey* for low pay.
- *Social Trends* (CSO) for wealth distribution.
- *The Annual Abstract of Statistics*, Inland Revenue and DHSS for tax rates, National Insurance rates and social security benefits.
- *Social Security Statistics* (DHSS) for information on claimants and benefits.
- International comparisons of living standards are based on an OECD report (*Times* 23 February 1983).
- Prices then and now are from each separate organisation —DHSS, BT etc.
- The estimated number on supplementary benefit in May 1982 (page 29) is from a written answer, *Hansard* 26 October 1982.

- Evidence on the poverty trap (page 30) is from *Taxing Credibility*, Low Pay Unit February 1983.
- The estimated loss to the unemployed (page 31) is from Jeff Rooker MP, 14 September 1982, based on House of Commons figures.
- The contrast between the DHSS crackdown, and laxity on tax is revealed in a DHSS press release 29 July 1982 and the *Financial Times* 19 November 1981.

4. Free Fire Zone in the Public Services ⎯⎯⎯⎯⎯⎯

The basic source is:

The *Government's Expenditure Plans* (GEP), (HMSO) 'The Public Spending White Paper' published each year giving detailed information on public spending programmes.

Education. Nursery education figures (page 36) are from Department of Education and Science (DES) statistical bulletins. Book provision figures are from the *HMI Report* on 'Effects of Local Authority Expenditure on Education 1981-2' and a report from the Educational Publishers' Council 25 January 1983. Evidence of inadequate provision (page 37) draws on the HMI Report, the *Cockcroft Report* on Mathematics in Schools 1981, DES Assessment of Performance Unit *Report* 1983 and DES figures. Evidence on school meals is from the *Report on School Meals* 30 July 1982, from the House of Commons Select Committee on Education. The University Grants Committee on the *State of Education* and a NATFHE Press Release October 1982 are the sources for cuts in higher education.

Health. Information on growing needs is given in the GEP. Evidence of cuts in maintenance (page 42) is from the *Report* of the House of Commons Select Committee on Social Services on the 1982 Public Expenditure White Paper. Regional imbalances were exposed in *The Guardian* 14 March 1983; underuse of hospital beds in a written answer, *Hansard* 16 March 1982; cuts in new developments in a special survey by the National Association of Health Administrators; lack of intensive care in *The Guardian* 3 December 1982, and possible savings on drugs in a Pharmaceutical Society Report published on 24 January 1983. The expansion of paybeds and private health is detailed in written answers, *Hansard* 3 March 1982 and 3 February

1982. Figures on the boom in health insurance are from Lee Donaldson Associates. Facts on NHS low pay are from COHSE 1982.

Transport. Rail facts are from British Rail, the Serpell Report and the BR statement *Rail Policy* 1981. Bus information is from the GEP, the Department of Employment, National Bus Company and the Department of Transport.

Personal Social Services. Information is drawn from reports published by the Association of Directors of Social Services, the GEP, Social Trends (CSO), and Report of the House of Commons Select Committee on Social Services in the 1982 Public Expenditure White Paper.

Housing. The dimensions of the housing crisis are revealed in the England and Wales *House Condition Surveys* 1981 and reports from the Building Research Establishment. Evidence of the cuts is found in the GEP and consequences for housebuilding in Department of the Environment (DoE) *Housing and Construction Statistics*. Statistics on rents are from the DoE, Chartered Institute of Public Finance and Accountancy, and DHSS social security statistics. The economics of council house sales (page 55) are derived from Parliamentary Questions and DoE Housing and Construction Statistics. The statistics for Housing Associations are from Housing Corporation *Annual Reports* and *Quarterly Bulletins*. Disrepair in the rented and owner-occupied sectors is revealed in the House Condition Surveys. Evidence of mortgage arrears (page 56) is given by V. Karn in *Roof*, Shelter 1983. Homelessness statistics are from the DoE. The slowdown in housing investment cuts and estimate of the backlog of repairs (page 57) is based on Association of Metropolitan Authorities analysis.

Privatisation. Information is from the *Financial Times* 24 September 1982; *Wimbledon News* 5 November 1982; *Labour Research* December 1981; *New Statesman* 2 February 1982; and *Privatisation and Public Services* GMWU 1982.

5. Rights Reduced

Information in this chapter is from government Acts, White Papers and Green Papers. Information on prisons is from Home Office statistics.

6. Life in the Eighties_____

Rural Areas. information is from *Farmers' Weekly* 21 November 1980, *Department of Employment Gazette*, and *State of the Countryside* 1982, *Rural Voice*.

Crime. The main source is *Criminal Statistics England and Wales*.

7. Britain in the World _____

Defence. Defence spending figures are from *The Government's Expenditure Plans* with international comparisons from NATO and Malcolm Chalmers (Bradford). Information on the nuclear weapons programme is from Malcolm Chalmers and Paul Rogers at the Bradford University School of Peace Studies. On military myths the sources are *The Times* 4 March 1983; Labour Party NEC Statement *Civil Defence*; *The Military Balance* 1982-3 by the International Institute for Strategic Studies; 'Nuclear Weapons in Europe' by Bill Arkin in *Disarming Europe*, Merlin 1982. On technology, US Government Information Agency Press Release 7 March 1983.

Aid. Information from *British Aid Statistics* and the Brandt Report: *North South—A Programme for Survival*, Pan 1980.

The Common Market. Figures are from the *Statement on the 1982 Community Budget* (Cmnd 8513), *Overseas Trade Statistics of the UK* (Department of Trade) and *Agriculture: The Triumph and the Shame* by Richard Body.

What the Tories have done to you

Women. Figures from Department of Employment Gazette (DEG), New Earnings Survey, and Economic Trends.

Black People. Figures from DEG June 1982, Commission for Racial Equality and Home Office report on racial attacks published in November 1981, and Valerie Karn, private communication.

Young People. Figures from DEG and the *Government's Expenditure Plans*.

Elderly People. Figures from House of Commons Select Committee on Social Services *Report on the 1982 Public Expenditure White Paper*.

Disabled People. Sources are DEG, Social Services Committee Report 1982, Shelter and a 1982 report by Richard Stowell for the Disablement Income Group.

Families with Children. Information drawn from *Making the First Last*, Frank Field MP, February 1983; DHSS *Social Security Statistics 1982*; *Taxing Credibility*, Low Pay Unit, February 1982; the Study Commission on the Family; *The Guardian* 11 March 1983 and 17 February 1983.

Index

SELF-SUFFICIENT BY 1981!!

THE PRIMEMINISTERIAL SCREAM